SEEING THROUGH YOUR ILLUSIONS

By Paul K. Chivington
With Laurel Elizabeth Keyes

G-L Publications
2168 South Lafayette
Denver, Colorado 80210

Third Printing

Published by G-L Publications
2168 S. Lafayette St.
Denver, Colo. 80210

Illustrations by Paul K. Chivington

Cover Design by Michelle Jones

To
All those remarkable people, who through
personal contact, or through their writings
have helped us see through our illusions.

Appreciation to Margaret Wilson
for her help in editing and proofing.

Other Books by the Authors

Paul K. Chivington
WHAT'S EATING YOU? (with Elizabeth Keyes)

Laurel Elizabeth Keyes
HOW TO WIN THE LOSING FIGHT
TONING—THE CREATIVE POWER OF THE VOICE
MYSTERY OF SEX
LIVING CAN BE FUN
CLOSE THE DOOR SOFTLY AS YOU GO
SUNDIAL
and others.

CONTENTS

INTRODUCTION

Why write another book?

Everything has been written about, and said over and over in many ways. Yet, with all of the books, people still are deceived, caught in endless illusions that result in suffering.

Is it possible that we have over-looked the Cause of this suffering?

It may be summed up in one word and that word is ILLU-SION. So, the way out of suffering may be simply to train the mind to see clearly the difference between illusion and reality in every facet of life—in relationships, beliefs, values and motivations.

To help people see their lives with new perspectives is the purpose of this book.

THE DAY
THE SUN STOOD STILL

"What the caterpillar calls the end of the world, the master calls a butterfly."

Richard Bach

1 I was waiting for the sun to come up.

Frost had formed on my sleeping bag where my breath had reached it. If I stretched or moved my body, it went out of the small area of body warmth and the shock of greater cold drew me back into the limitation of that comfort zone. Dawn in the high country can be miserable and one waits for the promise of light and relief that comes with the sun's first rays.

The sky was becoming steadily brighter as I watched. Up there above 10,000 feet in the Rockies the sky was vast, and as that great open dome spread its light with a relentless, constant increase, one felt dwarfed by comparison.

I watched.

Along with the other two Denver University engineering students, I was working during summer vacation surveying for timber access roads in the National Forest. It was the last of June, but the little stream beside our truck had a film of ice along the banks. The sharp, thin air cut into our lungs if we breathed deeply. We were waiting for the Forest Ranger to give the call to get up. Until that final moment of command, we huddled in our sleeping bags, waiting for the sun to announce that the day had begun.

I could estimate the exact place, in the crystal sky, where the sun would rise beyond the rugged peaks below us. I sighted it between the needles of a bristle cone pine branch.

It was coming up. I almost caught my breath waiting for the exact moment when its brilliance cut the earth and sky apart.

There it was! The sun. And, it moved amazingly fast as I measured it between the pine needles. It was no wonder that ancient people had said it climbed into the sky. Its movement was so unalterably steady that it was awesome.

Hadn't I ever seen a sunrise before, I asked myself a little sheepishly? Why this fascination with something that happened every day— had been happening every day for billions of years? Maybe this was the first time I had put all of my attention on it and watched it as something new, looking at it with fresh perspective.

"Get up, you guys," the Ranger called out.

We unzipped our sleeping bags and crawled out. However bad the pancakes might be, cooked on the makeshift grill, breakfast was welcome. From the blackened can that we used for a pot, tin cups filled with hot coffee warmed our hands as we held them. We sat on our haunches, close to the fire, trying to ignore the capricious smoke blowing around us as we ate.

"The sun is going to come up later everyday," the Ranger reminded us wryly, "days will be getting shorter now and we've got to get these roads finished before September.

We've got to make the time count."

Larry, who had taken a course in astronomy, made a statement that stopped all of us for a moment. "I'm going to make a prediction. The sun isn't going to come up tomorrow."

"What do you mean?"

"The sun is standing still. We're the ones turning toward it," he smiled smugly, having caught us off guard with his erudite comment.

The Ranger grunted, "Well, let's get turning toward the job and not waste any more time."

"That's my point," Larry persisted. "Most people see the sun moving and the earth standing still. It is more convenient to say what appears to be happening instead of what is really happening. Then we make rules that govern our lives out of unreal premises—like time, for instance. We make rules and then let them govern us."

His enlightening bit of philosophy was ignored and plans for the day's work were outlined. I was assigned to hack at brush while the others took the jeep up to a higher ridge. It gave me time in that mountain solitude to chase my earlier thoughts around.

Larry's comments haunted me. It might have been lack of oxygen in the high altitude that affected my brain, or that we had been cut off from any contact with civilization for days, but for the first time in my life I was acutely aware that I was on a great mass, turning toward a fixed object, a fiery ball of light. It was still. I was moving toward it. Yet I could *see* it moving and I could *feel* myself standing still. My senses were contradicting what I accepted intellectually.

At first I dismissed it. So what? It's no big deal. I *know* the truth.

Then I began to realize that such a simple oversight causes me to assume that I am at the center of the solar system. The universe appears to be revolving around me. That difference can present a grave problem in many calculations in my life.

Being an engineer, I don't like ambiguities. Why would an

intelligent human being relinquish a proven truth and opt for a well known illusion? "Know the truth and the truth shall set you free." The phrase popped into my mind. In the case of the sun, knowing the truth of its position and mine did not set me free from seeing an illusion.

It is convenient to say, "the sun is rising," or "setting." It is convenient because what is rotating happens to be us and we are too indifferent to make the adjustments from appearance to fact. Appearance wins out in our everyday living.

I stopped grubbing in the bushes and stood up, resting on my axe. Looking down across the range after range of mountains spreading out below me, it appeared that I was on top of the world. Nearby the spruce and fir trees were vividly green. The next range was a softer color. The distant ones became purple and finally a faint smoky blue. I accepted those definitions of purple and blue, knowing full well that all of the trees were dark green. How much of our world did we see falsely because it was easier to accept a sense perception than to think through to reality?

Close to my boots I noticed an ant hill that my digging had disturbed. I looked at ants scurrying around. They had no awareness that the earth they were on was round, or moving. Their level of perception limited their ability to see any further than a few inches so their world was only a few yards in dimension. That is all right for ants because they will never leave the earth so it is sufficient to be comfortable in what is familiar. If an ant could take a ruler and measure the earth an inch at a time, it would conclude that the earth was flat. But when man assumes that the earth is flat he limits his own evolution. If he tried to hold to that flat-earth idea, he would never succeed in going into space, put up satellites or expand his thinking. To expand his world, man had to make an effort to see and think past the deceptions his senses gave him.

Around me there was no sound but an occasional gust of wind in the trees, and now and then a bird call. The bigness of it all, and the aloneness, pressed in on me to dig for answers as ruthlessly as I had dug brush roots and rocks from the mountain's hold.

We finished the trails that season. They had only a slight semblance of roads, but they could be used. That was the way I felt about this new world of ideas regarding Truth and Reality that the summer experience had opened up for me; not smooth, paved highways of thought but trails that would get me where I intended to go.

The impact of these illusions remained with me during the years in aero-space work, designing computers, working with bio-medical equipment and into the study of holography. In that I began to find answers. Yet, even with answers, it was hard to retrain my thinking and break out of the old flat-earth systems, the Newtonian restrictions, and begin to function in a realm of wholeness.

For example: Join me in a little exercise. You are reading this book. It appears to be solid. In fact it is mostly not here at all. Analyzed under a microscope the pages become visible wood fibers. Under an electron microscope the space between the fibers is very evident. Further analysis to the molecular level shows the space increases and the particles begin to fade. Below the atomic structure the particles fade into probability patterns of energy. These patterns of energy fall into many categories, one of which is called a *quark*, an essential building block of matter. However, there is a catch to that. We have never seen a quark. We take it on faith. So this book exists on the belief that quarks exist and therefore this book exists based on your faith in quarks.

But, you can hold it and read it. It is *convenient* to assume that it is a real object.

As you begin to take a second look at a "thing" or the objective world, you realize that "thinging" is convenient. To think of the world as made up of waves of energy vibrating at different frequencies may be the fact but it is out of favor in our here-now everyday living. "Waving" suggests that the objects we label as "things" may only be vibrations. It is similar to the plucking of a string on a violin. It will vibrate into a sound but we cannot see the vibration.

It works something like this: If we wish to see a universe made up of things then everywhere we look we will see things of different sizes and shapes, objects separated from us. On the other hand if we wish to see a universe made up of vibrating energy at different frequencies, the universe becomes an energy system, unobstructed and limitless.

Case in point: LIGHT

Visible light is the very small portion of the broader electromagnetic spectrum. However, it behaves in a peculiar manner. Sometimes it appears to be made up of small packets of energy called photons. These react like things or *particles*. At other times light appears to be made of *waves* which have totally different characteristics when compared to particles. Are both descriptions of light correct? Absolutely.

How can a phenomenon, such as light, be described correctly in two opposite terms? Many orthodox scientists feel uncomfortable in the presence of ambiguities and paradoxes. They are clinging desperately to the material world hoping the world of unexplainable events, that is the paranormal, will go away and not challenge their archaic theories.

It becomes apparent that the universe itself is a paradox. It is energy that can be seen as both particle and wave. What is comforting about all this is that our brains were designed to resolve paradoxes.

Example: THE BOX

The brain responds to the world of patterns (events) by choosing a perspective with which to view that pattern. *By choosing a perspective it sets into motion a feedback system which reinforces that perspective.*

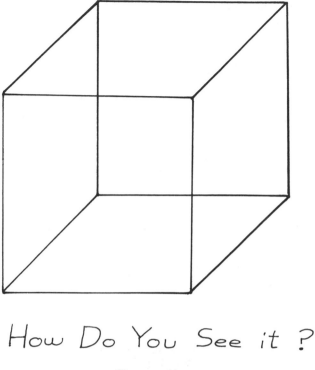

How Do You See it ?

(Figure 1)

Here is a pattern of dark lines on white paper.

I select a perspective of those lines which creates the image of a box. I could ignore the box, and choose to see an undefined pattern of intersecting lines. The choice is mine. I am more accustomed to seeing them as a "box".

When I choose to see a box the box suddenly takes form. It extends out from the page and reinforces my selection. Without changing anything on the paper, a box has been created for me to see. A 3D box, one with depth.

Next I will change my perspective. I see that the front surface has moved to the back, and the back has become the front. It appears at first to be lying on its side, with the opening in front. Now it has changed to an upright position with the opening at the top.

Nothing on the page has changed but the box has completely reversed its position in my mind. What caused the box to change—to flip from one position to another?

I did!

Did the box appear to change all of its lines to support my chosen perspective? Yes.

Did it change from one orientation to the other slowly? No.

The change was instantaneous and it took place inside my brain.

Then, *it appears that the brain is where my world is being created*. It isn't "out there." It is "in here," in my own head.

If you have difficulty in seeing the box flip, try this easier picture. Here is a pattern of dark and light regions. You can detect the dark portion as a vase. (Odd, isn't it, how we seem to see the dark segments before the white?) Now, look for two white faces, opposing each other. The principle is the same. It is an "either or" process, for we can't seem to see both at once.

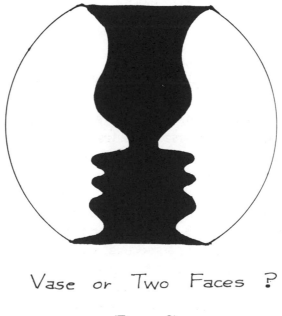

Vase or Two Faces ?

(Figure 2)

You choose to give meaning to one set of lines or the other and the brain obeys your decision to see it as you wish. Could we say this seems to be a fact of life? We see what we decide to see, giving it the meaning we wish to put upon it.

There is always more than one perspective to any given occurrence or pattern.

It is a configuration of units of energy.

It is good, therefore it is right.

It is bad, therefore wrong.

Or, we may define it as—

It is mine, therefore it is right. Because it is my idea, I will defend it.

It is theirs, therefore it is wrong and a threat to me.

It is too much for me to comprehend so I'll just say it is "God's Will."

All have validity since each one depends upon one's determination to create it as he sees it. It reflects a particular journey through life. The journey depends on where the person has come from, what values and opinions have been formed, and where that one is going with the decisions and convictions directing the brain to form images.

The important factor to remember is this: When you have chosen a particular perspective on life, don't be surprised when it turns out to be just that way for you. Always allow for the fact that someone else may be choosing a totally different perspective, and the universe will rush in to greet him from that point of view. Or, so it seems to him.

What is really going on here?

It all depends on what is going on inside our brains. The world we live in is one which we create by interpreting patterns of energy in an infinite variety of ways.

That summer in the Forest Service was just the beginning of my attempt to see through illusions.

THE FIVE
MESSENGERS OF ILLUSION

The material world consists of many layers of energy patterns, all but one of which appears out of focus to our five senses. Thus we register that single layer of energy patterns as the REAL world.

2 Having realized that everything I perceive may not be as it appears, I began asking the question—"What is real?" How much of my reality is created in my brain, and how much is really "out there"?

Most of the information that we have comes through the five senses. This is called empirical science. If they are all illusions, how can I have learned anything from them? There must be a way to sort out *reality* from *illusion*.

I imagined that I was locked inside of a dark room with two windows, and two speakers with microphones hooked up in the room. In addition, I had two mechanical arms and hands that could reach outside the room to inform me about the outside world. Adding the ability to taste and smell, I had crudely described the senses which receive impressions and interpret the world in which I live, in my brain.

How accurate are these messengers? "Seeing is believing." "But, I heard it." "I touched it, I know it's there." The infallible senses? They can fool us completely.

SEEING

We have seen magicians use slight of hand to deceive the sight-believers. The eye clearly sees something that may not be there in objective form. The reason is that we don't see just with the eyes. We see with our brains. The image of the world stops at the back of the eyeball where it becomes a series of complicated electrochemical signals. The brain knows how to put these signals back together to form a picture—a sunset or a Mona Lisa. The brain responds to some command we have given it but we don't know how it operates.

We do know how we feel about something. That feeling can change the way we see a thing. A different picture is formed in the brain. This is why two individuals can observe the same object and describe quite different accounts of it.

One of the miracles is that we can see at all. Seeing isn't a simple photographic technique of focusing the lens of the eye so that the image falls properly on the retina and then the image races up a fiber optic tube to some photographic film in the brain, called memory cells, where pictures are stored. Not at all.

At the back of the eyeball are light sensitive rods and cones which translate photons of light into nerve impulses which leave the eyeball in a bundle of nerves. This bundle is the *optic tract*. If we could open up the optic tract and look inside we would see a complex grouping of nerves. If we could look inside those nerves, while the person was watching a ball game or a landscape, we would find no pictures at all.

What would appear would resemble static on a TV screen

when the picture is lost. What happened to the picture? It had been transformed into a frequency domain. Those little electrochemical pulsations are all coded and the brain takes them and transforms them into what the person *thinks* he is seeing, the ball game or landscape.

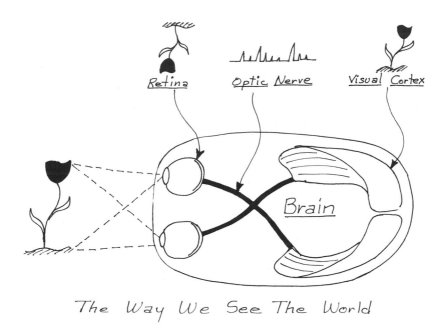

The Way We See The World

Figure 3

Marvelous as it is, the eye can see only through a very small window of the electromagnetic spectrum called the visible spectrum. (There is much more that it can't see yet we know that it exists.)

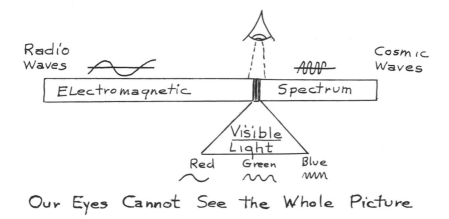

Our Eyes Cannot See the Whole Picture

Figure 4

With this limited view of the world of light it is no wonder that our ideas of the universe have been limited. Imagine what it would be like if we could see all of the radio and TV signals passing through the room in one moment. We would explode, probably, from sensory overload—blow a fuse.

The process of seeing is similar to the deep space probe cameras used in gathering pictures from Mars, Jupiter and Saturn. Highly sensitive cameras converted visual images into a series of electrical pulses so coded that after being transmitted back to earth they could be reassembled into a photograph. We consider it something of a miracle that we can take pictures of a far away Jupiter moon or Saturn's rings, but we use a similar process every time we use our eyes.

An incredible number of electrical pulses are required for one picture taken of anything in outer space. The resulting computer printout is complicated, and leaves much to be desired. Our eyes do much better than our best technology every time we read a word of print. They not only transform marks on paper into an image of a picture, but also change that image into electrical pulses that somehow change into the picture we imagined!

Who wrote the program, coded it, reassembled it to make sense?

What about DNA patterns and inherited qualities? Who/What is deciding what it wishes to see and gives it meaning?

It might be easier to trust the whole thing up to some idea of a Creator, instead of trying to figure it out for ourselves. But our brains were constructed to feed upon new information. Curiosity is vital to keeping them in good condition. So, even as we tumble and whirl in the new dimensions of space, we try to grasp and hold on to bits of information.

If what we encounter in our waking state of seeing isn't confusing enough, what about what we "see" in the dream state? Is that real or illusion? Every night when we enter REM (Rapid Eye Movement) sleep, and begin dreaming we are re-structuring the coded system into brilliant 3D pictures with no further input to the eyeball from outside. What is seeing them? Apparently it isn't the eye. Those pictures are being re-formed and seen somewhere in the brain.

It has been agreed that over 80% of what we consider "reality" depends on what we see, and now it appears that it is our most powerful messenger of illusion.

HEARING

Perhaps we will find that hearing is a more reliable messenger. Right off, we find our sense of hearing is inferior to that of animals in many instances. The human ear can respond to sound vibrations from approximately twenty cycles per second to 20,000. But sound, the vibration of air molecules on the eardrum, vibrates far higher and lower than the ear can detect. Again, it is amazing that we can hear at all. Just as light passes through vitreous humor of the eyeball, sound passes through fluid in the *Organ of Corti* located in the *cochlea,* or inner ear.

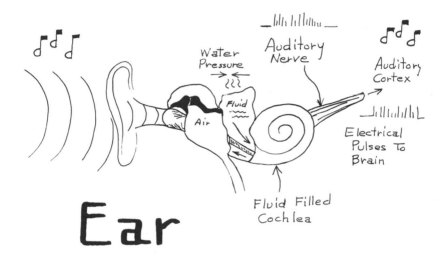

Figure 5

Both light and sound must pass through a fluid chamber before being detected by the appropriate nerve receptors. The beautiful, complicated sound patterns that we hear in music come to us through liquid.

How can sound deceive?

When you listen to a stereo system, the two speakers, separated by a distance of six or eight feet, bring combined sound to us from what seems to be a place between the speakers. The speakers have to be phased accurately to give the impression of a phantom source in between the two speakers.

If you tried to listen to a favorite composition while you held your ears under water, you would appreciate the remarkable operation that goes on automatically within the auditory cortex of the brain, and how it resonates on the lobes of the brain. All sound, music, speech or whatever, is received by us through the electrochemical nerve impulses coming from tiny hairs floating in the fluid of the Organ of Corti. They are received and interpreted by an area of the brain called the auditory cortex.

To help you appreciate the magic of what goes on in your brain through the sense of hearing, remember when you have answered the telephone and heard a voice that you have not heard for years? In a fraction of a second, you recognized that voice and conjured up a picture of the person belonging to it. How did you do that?

No matter how you might try, you would not be able to describe that particular voice to me so that I could recognize it the first time I heard it.

Your brain used frequency analysis. That is another term for explaining that it works with frequency ratios of nerve impulses, not sounds.

To further complicate the situation, we do not always record exactly what we hear. Since the brain performs selective listening, there will always be arguments or disagreements, divorces and wars. The fact is, that our brains have a talent for shifting sounds around, like the lines in the box illustration, to agree with what we wish to hear—and drop the rest of the sound completely.

Another instance of illusion: While you are reading this book, stop and listen to the sounds around you. Is the clock ticking, a horn honking, a faucet dripping, or a child shouting? These sounds may be continuous in the background. Your ears hear them, but you do not notice them because you are intent on the material you are reading.

(A test of your interest in this book is—did you notice these sounds before I mentioned them? I hope not!)

TOUCHING

Your sight may be tricked and your hearing deceived, but if you touch something you know that it is really there. Is it?

Dr. Karl Pribram, a neuropsychologist at Stanford University, talks about the experiment that was performed with several fine tuning forks vibrating on the forearm.[1] When the vibrations were phased properly, the sense of touch recorded only a single point of vibration, though there were several contacts with tuning forks along the skin. Again, phasing of signals is the key to forming an illusion.

The strength of a touch does not, in itself, transmit a message. A friend may give a man a hearty slap on the back, and it is accepted as an affectionate gesture. If in an argument, even a slight push may be interpreted as offensive, a hard blow.

An old test is to plunge the hand into a container of hot water, then into another of icy water, and for a few seconds the cold water seems to be burning.

Touch is a most important sense, especially to the young child who grows emotionally handicapped when denied normal touch contact with a mother figure. It can be a language of itself in communicating sympathy, tenderness, affection, aggression or anger, according to the meaning we give it.

Dr. Manfred Clynes explained the remarkable sensitivity of touch in his book, *Sentics, The Touch Of Emotions*. An almost imperceptible movement of the fingers can register a wide range of emotions, especially in the response to music and color. Dr. Clynes had discovered a little known fact that we impart our feelings by the manner in which we touch, yet discerning as this sense is, touch cannot register the molecules of space between the atoms in this page. It gives a limited perspective of a very complex world.

SMELLING

Here we have the oldest and supposedly most reliable sense. Its purpose was primarily for survival, and mating, in the animal world. A predator could hide in the darkness, making no sound at all, but its scent would reveal its presence. It is the sense most associated with sexual arousal—from the musk deer to the perfume on a woman's dressing table, scents seem to provide a powerful stimulus. Perhaps this is because it is the only sense that is not evaluated in the cortex of the brain. It has its own center, the olfactory area, and does not respond to the odor itself, but to the electrochemical impulses triggered by the scent in the air.

Smell can be a signal of disorder and ill health, both mental and physical. Some people insist that they can smell death, or the approach of death in an ill person.

It is very real to them for decay sends out unpleasant odors. It is recognized that emotionally disturbed people give off an unpleasant, dank and cloying smell that clings to a room even after they have left it.

Can smell be deceptive? Apparently it can be. Science has recently discovered a peculiar chemical substance given off by males which acts on the female brain in a way that makes her want to be with him. The substance is called *pheromone*. Many large perfume manufacturers have cashed in on this reaction by putting pheromones in their products. Some women have cried, "foul!" They claim it is a deceptive method of influencing their behavior. They might find themselves irresistibly attracted to a man who otherwise would repulse them. Who's deceiving whom?

TASTING

This sense is associated closely with smell, intended to guide our selection of food. It detects four qualities; sweet, sour, bitter and salty. Even with smell to guide us, taste can easily be fooled. Taste should be our safeguard to good nourishment, but we have let it fool us to the extent that if we relied on it alone we would let it kill us. We will eat almost anything that tastes what we decide is "good". Modern living habits have destroyed the natural selectivity of taste buds. Smoking dulls the taste buds, of course. Many hot and spicy flavors do the same thing. Over-planting has depleted the soil and that along with picking green, immature fruits and vegetables so that they will hold up in shipping has destroyed much of the flavor they had originally. Subsequently, manufacturers compensate for this by adding sweetening and spices to almost everything that is to be consumed, to artificially stimulate the taste buds. From baby food to catsup, sugar is added to make the taste enticing. This is such a common practice that most children are sugar addicts by the time they are eight years old. Taste buds have become so abused by false flavors that people refuse natural, ripened food that a body needs for good health, choosing instead the highly seasoned, greasy (for fat sustains flavors) and depleted substitutes.

Our sense of taste was intended to guide our appetites so we would have proper nourishment to satisfy our hunger. Instead, we have let taste deceive us into ignoring hunger for the body's needs and it dictates our choices for its own pleasure.

SENSE EXTENSION

We have extended our senses, as tools for investigating and learning, but we have not extended our understanding of reality. We extend sight with telescopes and microscopes, sound with speaker amplifiers and microphones. By remote control, a touch can swing a huge earth-moving vehicle around as easily as stirring a spoon in a cup. The telescope extended our vision of the universe but permitted us to look only backwards in time. Television has enabled us to see across our planet at the speed of light but has not dispelled illusions. Rather, it has multiplied them. Most of the information we receive deals with violence, tragedy, terrorism and even entertainment is based on holding attention by its shock value so the sponsors can sell their products to an entranced audience. These frightening portrayals are committed by about one percent of its population but the messages we receive indicate that almost everyone in the world is behaving in that manner.

Technology of sound reproduction is another highly deceptive area. On one hand it has provided us with flawless reproduction of the great classics in music. On the other hand, it has provided rock performers with electric equipment so intensified that it is destroying our hearing and even damaging buildings and killing plant life.

According to research by the Better Hearing Institute, Washington, D.C., these figures were given for "continuous exposure time permitted before *hearing damage.*"

Average home	50 decibels	Time—no limit
Average car	70 decibels	Time—no limit
Power mower	105 decibels	Time—1 hour
Rock band	115 decibels	Time—*15 minutes!*

Most teenagers have impaired hearing to some extent before they leave high school, and permanent deafness is in store for a large part of our population because they have permitted so-called entertainment to destroy the delicate mechanism of hearing.

Extending the senses mechanically may be exciting but it does not break the illusions.

BREAKING THROUGH THE SENSE BARRIERS

There are two important steps we must take to break through the cloud of illusions. The first step involves *refinement* of the senses. The second step necessitates going behind the senses to find the *observer* and *interpreter* of illusion.

If you follow through on this idea you will see illusion crumbling away and exposing a new world of reality, one which gives you immense freedom and peace of mind.

REFINEMENT OF THE SENSES

This is a most controversial topic in our society. What is refined? In fact, the very word, "refinement," is considered obsolete by many people.

There are courses given in universities, clubs and businesses as well as lectures and workshops endorsed for social workers and counselors for the purpose of making people insensitive. Supposedly so they won't be hurt by living in our complex world; so that they can be totally self-interested and indifferent to others. The goal seems to be to make one immune to shock or compassion. Vulgarities, obscenities, violence and cruelty all numb sense registry. Consequently, when you are walking down the street and see someone being attacked you won't respond with feelings of horror or helpfulness. You may become so schooled in insensitivity that you pride yourself on not being moved by anything. You will live in a sterile little shell of non-involvement and cold indifference.

The idea should be not to deaden the senses but to be selective—to use them as tools and not be enslaved by them.

Can this attitude, so common among us now, caused by coarse vibrations entering the brain through sight and sound, be changed? Of course. It is a matter of taking charge of our choices. Begin to stand back and recognize the gross sensations before letting them "in" to register on your brain. Instead of waiting for block-busters to knock you around, look for the subtle and beautiful. Subtlety is a way of life in Oriental cultures. Japan, India and other Eastern people use politeness and diplomacy as tools for survival. *Just plain consideration for others should be the basis of all civilized conduct.*

REFINING SIGHT

Be selective in your viewing diet. Say "no" to the enticing advertisement of a violent, horror film intended to shock your nervous system and scare you half to death. Ask yourself why you should subject your eyes, ears, brain and

body to that kind of harmful treatment. Choose to see programs or films that rely on wholesomeness and naturalness,
and are informative and humorous. This is the first step—be
aware and choose.

What type of art do you have hanging on the walls of your
home or office? Is it beautiful and inspiring, based on right
proportion, or is it distorted, inconsistent and depressing?
There is a right proportion used in nature in all flower and
plant patterns. We find this in the *Golden Section*, which
served as a guide to the great masterpieces, especially since
the book, with Leonardo daVinci's illustrations was published in 1509. Leonardo Fibonacci, one of the greatest
mathematicians of the Middle Ages, brought to light the ancient Egyptian mathematical progression of numbers:
1—2—3—5—8—13—21, etc.,) which was related to the
remarkable dimensions of the pyramids.[2] These were
acknowledged reflections of natural law or the natural
physics upon which our worlds were fashioned and whatever
is constructed on those proportions gives energy, through
beauty and harmony, to the perceivers. Pythagoras, with the
same idea, based beauty on these harmonic proportions.[3] He
said, "God geometricizes." Great masterpieces in music are
conceived on similar proportions, as are the *Ragas* in Indian
music that have remained unchanged through thousands of
years.

Much of the architecture built at the founding of our nation
came from the same pattern, through Jefferson and others of
that era. They were familiar with Masonic teachings that carried on the ancient Hermetic (and Egyptian) concepts. Even
the graceful furniture of that period reflected curved, clean
lines and right proportions of the congruent patterns of
mathematics and physics.

While Laurel Keyes was doing a workshop for a
psychiatrist's patients recently, she was invited to his home
and was most impressed by the pictures he lived with there.
All were copies of fine old masters. When she commented
on this, he replied, "Our subconsious is fed by our surroun-

dings. We may not consciously see the picture after a time but our subconscious registers it every time we pass it, and it does have a definite influence on the decisions we make and our attitudes and general life style."

Pictures of tortured feelings, angry sharp lines and glaring or ugly colors are making statements to us whenever we are in their presence. They may be expressions of someone's anger and despair, and may portray those emotions very well but ask yourself if you want those emotions to enter your life—do you want to feel like that?

One of our friends studied with Dr. Carl Jung. He told her that he encouraged disturbed patients to paint to get rid of their dark emotions, "but then the pictures should be destroyed. Once they are out, one should not continue to live with them."

Refinement of visual sense takes conscious effort. The rewards are all worth the effort. After you have practiced it for some time you will notice that your sight is extending into a realm you had not been aware of before. More than that your THINKING is extended to better areas. You seek more amicable relationships and you expect better results from whatever you do. Hope follows inspiration. Enthusiasm follows hope and you will find that you are creating a more beautiful and congenial world in which to live.

You will begin to see subtle energy patterns around objects and people. You won't need to ask a person about his intentions or motives because you will sense them directly. Regardless of what a person says, you will know what he feels. Wouldn't all of us like to be able to do this? We can if we will begin to refine the sense of sight.

A sadhu from India said about refinement; "We were fine to begin with but got coarsened. Now we go back to refining ourselves."

REFINING SOUND

How does refinement apply to sound?

This is one of the most difficult senses for most people to

refine. The illusions resulting from over stimulation are very hard to resist. Also, the entrance of sound vibrations is not limited to the ear—it penetrates every cell of the body and influences the emotions more than any other sense. Often, it bypasses intellectual control and even when one decides not to respond to a lively march, the moment the attention is withdrawn the foot begins to tap

Drum beats were recognized by early man to increase the heart beat and raise the feelings of hostility, causing the listeners to want to fight. Drums and marching music are a part of war preparations because they do heighten emotions. Football and other competitive games are accompanied by that type of music. It excites the audience as well as goading the players.

A study has been made relating highway accidents to music on car radios. It was found that rock music caused drivers to be more aggressive and irritable, with heavier foot on the throttle. It is a standing joke among used car salesmen that if the setting on the car radio is on a rock station the odds are that the transmission is about to go out. Here in Colorado, we have had several murders resulting from traffic disputes; something as simple as a car cutting in front of another, accidentally or within legal limits, caused a driver to be outraged. Ramming of the car or confrontation often results in shots or stabbings. This was unheard of a few decades ago. Some 1500 years ago, Cassiodorus wrote in his *Divine Letters*, "Music doth extenuate fears and furies, and it can appease cruelty and causeth quiet rest." (Depending on the type of music.)

A story told by a missionary in Africa illustrates that very well. He played semi-classical music to a tribe that had never heard white man's music before. Members of the tribe listened and were pleased, smiling and nodding their heads in approval. Then, without comment, the missionary played acid rock music. Immediately, they reacted. They became agitated. They threw rocks at the record player, obviously trying to kill the threatening thing.[4]

Plants react to music. Experiments done in Colorado Womans College by Dorothy Retallack were reported in her book, *The Sound of Music and Plants*. They showed that the molecular structure was affected by the music played. Roots were shallow and the plant grew away from the sound of rock music, bending as much as 90°. Sturdy geraniums, twelve inches high, died as completely as if a flame thrower had been turned on them. The same decibel level was used for all types of music. (Had the sound been louder the plants would have died sooner, undoubtedly.) It was the rhythm that seemed to make such a difference—the monotonous beat or syncopated, choppy rhythms were disastrous to the life force in the plants. When melodious or concordant classical compositions were played, the root structure was strong, and the plants leaned toward the sound and grew much taller. Plants do not have opinions, and are not conditioned by mental concepts. This was just the result of damage or enrichment to the cell structure. Human cells must react in a similar manner.[5]

There are other studies that indicate certain types of rhythm in modern music contribute to weakening of the body and produce stress.

Refinement of the sense of hearing, then, can begin with selecting melodic, inspiring sounds. There are numerous cassettes now of natural sounds, of the ocean, mountain streams, bird songs and other sounds of nature that smooth away our stress and tensions. Gregorian chants and Baroque music in particular are renewing rather than destructive. Lively tunes may be found in early English music, and are also renewing to us.

In the book, *Super Learning*, the authors list the types of music which enhance better learning.[6] The brain appears to function more efficiently when processing a particular type of music. This music is largely Baroque. (Handel, Mozart, Vivaldi, Bach, etc.). Dr. Steve Halpern has produced some of our best modern music, *Spectrum Suite*, *Dawn* and others. *Golden Voyage* by Ron Dexter is another example of music that nourishes and restores our emotional nature. Flutist James Galway takes us into other dimensions of experience when we listen to his *Song of the Seashore*. These are just a few to give an idea of the excellent music that is available.

The emotions are so easily directed by music. Sad or joyous music swings us along with its moods because we tune into the consciousness of the composers. This was clearly established by Clynes' experiments, (mentioned earlier). As a listener of music, are you tuning into the consciousness of a composer who saw the unity and beauty of life, or one whose life consisted of dissipation through drugs and alcohol? Some Negro spirituals were deeply moving but they portrayed sorrow and entrapment. To listen to them for long periods of time puts us into the same mental and emotional state of deprivation and hopelessness. The music talks to the subconscious mind. Words alone can not lift a heavy beat into beneficial influence. Churches are being deceived when they use rock music with pretty, religious words. It is the beat that will move the hearers to a baser emotional response, by-passing the intention of the words. Discordant, heavy-beat sounds stimulate violent feelings. What you take "in" through your senses will eventually come out through your actions. If you don't take it in—it isn't a part of your world.

REFINING TOUCH

Touch is a sense modality that has great potential when refined.

What do I mean by "refined" touch? Have you ever watched a mother stroke the feverish face of her child? The reassuring arm placed around someone's shoulder when they needed comforting? The gentle placing of a hand on that of someone tenderly loved? These are refined expressions of touch. It can be a more powerful medium of communication than any word.

These touches are the opposite of the pushing, shoving or slapping which separates one from another. The heavy "stroking" and mauling practices which have become popular in some therapy classes may be acceptable to the animal nature of the body but they can not be considered refinement of the sense of touch. Anything that invades the privacy of a person tends to desensitize rather than refine.

L.K. tells of having tea with a Japanese family and commenting on the delicate, egg-shell thin cups being used. The aged grandmother replied, "Yes, they have been in daily use in my family for nearly a hundred years." That is an example of refined handling! Compare that use to the heavy, stoneware, dishwasher proof, clunky dishes so popular in our society. Do they reflect our heaviness and carelessness of touch?

Sexual encounters are perfect examples of the touch expression. Grabbing, clutching and thrusting at another's body will eventually cause repulsion. Sexual expression using a gentle touch to express love draws each one closer to the other. The Tantric system of love making has closely adhered to this awareness for over a thousand years. It works.[7]

What is the benefit of this refined touching? First, you will notice that you are more sensitive to the message of another's touch. You will be able to understand that person's feelings directly without saying anything.

Second, you will notice your hands have a radiating energy of their own. You will find that you can impart what might be called healing energy through them. The sense of touch is an expression of the heart. Learn to express these feelings closer to "reality."

REFINING SMELL
Smell is a sense which has become so dulled that many people aren't aware of it at all. Have you ever gone into a house and been assailed by unpleasant odors? If you tried, you could trace it down to stacks of dirty dishes left in the kitchen sink, unemptied ash trays, accumulated soiled clothing or stale cooking odors. House members didn't notice them

because they were accustomed to them.

Probably nothing is so appealing as the smell of something *clean*. And, the natural fragrances of fresh flowers, baked bread right from the oven, linens brought in from being sun-dried in the wind, the forest after rain and the moist skin of a sleeping child. All appeal to a refined sense of smell.

Again, to refine that sense as any sense, one must first be aware—then choose the finer expression of it.

There are some individuals who give off a pleasant scent without using perfumes or deodorants. They live very refined lives. A very religious couple, who rented a house from me, left a lingering fresh flower fragrance there when they moved. And, L. K. tells of a holy man whom she visited in a mountain cabin, in winter time, and the place was permeated with the scent of roses.

REFINING TASTE

Another sense to refine is taste. Basically, we are talking about refining our taste in foods. Notice I said "refining our taste in foods," not tasting refined foods. Attitudes, emotions and actions can often be traced back to the choice one has made of food.

For example: Sugar can cause one to feel depressed and exhausted after the temporary lift it has given. Much red meat in the diet stimulates feelings of aggression—perhaps because our intestinal tract was not fashioned to digest meat, as the dog or lion, and it causes irritation and distress. It is very difficult to be patient and a good listener when the pulse is pounding after three or four cups of coffee or other caffeine drinks.

By choosing fresh, uncooked fruits and vegetables and nuts, natural grains and (if they are available) natural dairy products and eggs, and eliminating junk and processed foods with many added chemicals, we are taking a big step toward taste refinement.

Some doctors were astonished when schizophrenic patients who used dialysis machines for kidney disorders lost their schizoid tendencies. Cleansing of the blood removed the substance that had triggered the brain to behave erratically. The blood feeds the brain. If it is filled with toxins and chemicals how can we expect the brain to respond coherently?

Refine the selections of foods you eat. This process can be more clearly understood by reading *What's Eating You?*, the book I co-authored with Elizabeth Keyes.

If we can bring each of the five senses into coherence, the brain will begin to break through the illusions and see the world as a place of more harmony and beauty and consistency.

GOING BEHIND THE SENSES

The process of refinement is two-fold. First is to refine the input to the senses. Second is to go behind the senses and meet your Observer.

Who/What is the Observer?

Ask yourself who is reading this page? Is it your eyes? (We have already established that you see with your brain.) If I could put you to sleep and open your eyelids you would *not* see this page immediatley. No! You would first have *to become conscious*, orient yourself to where you are and what you saw before you. Seeing requires conscious effort and direction.

Everyone has had the experience, while reading something, of having the mind go off on another thought process. Maybe a paragraph or two is read by the eyes but we cannot remember a single word of it. The consciousness is not fastened to what the eye is seeing. In this common wandering of the mind there is proof that there is *something* behind the eyes that can see separately from their observation.

Behind every sensory stimulation there is an INTERPRETER. This interpreter gives meaning and value to sense stimulation. In fact, it chooses to allow it to be registered by the brain or not.

You become master of your life when you recognize a very simple law of physics. "All phenomena is energy in vibration." You label it "good" or "bad", "right" or "wrong" based on your feelings about the manifestation.

Some time ago I had the experience of spending an hour in a sensory deprivation tank. This is a device which looks like a coffin with salt water in the lower portion of the box.

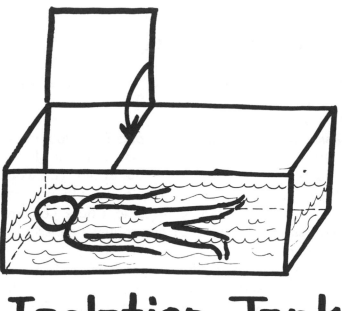

Isolation Tank

Figure 6

I opened the lid, stepped inside, closed the lid and began to float on the water. My body was suspended, so I had no sensation of gravity affecting my sense of touch. Inside, it was absolutely dark and silent. My senses were without any input to feed my brain.

At first there was a moment almost of panic, and then I began to ask myself, "Who am I?" Without my senses to define my body I had to redefine myself.

The next event that happened was that I became aware of my mind chattering away about past memories. With considerable conscious effort, I told my mind to shut up. Suddenly I was cognizant of the fact that I WAS. I was just BE-ING. There were no stimulations, no illusions—just pure consciousness.

It was a wonderful feeling. I realized that I was in charge of this melodrama that I called my life and if I didn't like the script I could change it.

Time ceased. I was aware of being there but without a body. I had been told that after an hour someone would come to open the lid and help me out but I had no idea of the passage of time at all. Is there a message here about the tie between time and sensation?

When I came out of the tank, I felt thoroughly refreshed. I looked about me and found that my seeing was different. Hearing was different. Each of my senses became like tools or extensions of my consciousness. However, I felt strangely separate from them.

I stumbled on the step leading down from the chamber. My toe was stubbed and hurt but I didn't hurt—my toe did. I was not my toe or the hurt. It was a feeling of experiencing and yet not being identified with the experience. I apologized to my body for being clumsy and went out the door.

From that day I have been constantly aware of the Observer who is within me. He simply makes notes of how I get all caught up in a football game, or a movie which is well done, or an exciting scientific article that I read but I am still mindful of who is getting caught up in the illusion.

This is a major step in breaking through the illusion. If you don't understand that the world you have created is all illusion, you can easily become a slave to any or all of your five senses. They can be either shackles or wings. Understanding your refinement of senses and bringing senses into coherence will give you freedom you have not known before.

The five senses, then, become messengers of reality instead of deception. It is worth the effort to cultivate them as tools to create a better life for yourself.

HOLOGRAPHY—
THE ULTIMATE ILLUSION

"Just as a stone flung into the water becomes the center and cause of many circles, and as sound diffuses itself in circles in the air, so any object, placed in the luminous atmosphere, diffuses itself in circles and fills the surrounding air with infinite images of itself. And is repeated, the whole everywhere, and the whole in every smallest part."

Leonardo da Vinci

3 In the summer of 1965, I was busy meeting schedule deadlines for the checkout equipment for the Saturn Moon Rocket. The team with which I was working was exceptionally talented. North American Space & Information Systems, as it was known then, was a prime contractor for the Saturn Rocket and Apollo Space Craft.

One day during lunch, a group of fellow engineers and I were talking about hobbies. One of them was working with photography. He was excited about a new type of photography using the LASER (Light Amplification through Stimulated Emission of Radiation). It was called holography. His source was an article in *Scientific American* (June '65), about the three dimensional effect of this new discovery and its ultimate application to 3D television.

In 1972 I came across the subject again. This time it was an actual film on holography. By then I was working for Hughes Aircraft in Los Angeles. Each year the West Coast hosts a Western Electronic Conference for engineering companies. The purpose is to educate the engineering community about new developments and the state of the art in technology. In addition to the hardware and software displayed, at this conference, there was a Science Theatre which previewed the year's ten best science films. These films were not the Star Wars type, although they were futuristic. They were more technical and informative than entertaining. The title of one of the films caught my attention. "Holography, Window of the Future." It was produced by The Veterans Administration in Washington, D.C.

Here was my chance to see what this new development in photography was all about.

As I entered the Science Theatre that afternoon, I felt the anticipation of experiencing a new discovery. This was a familiar process, for my going from vacuum tubes to transistors and then to integrated circuits and finally to microprocessors kept me learning at all times. It was part of my job to be alert to technological growth.

The film ran about thirty minutes. At the end of it, I sat in the darkened room feeling numb. What I had just seen was not only a new technique in photography, it was a mind-expanding experience dealing with the world of illusion and reality.

The first half of the film dealt with the physics of light and the theory of holography. The second half was filmed in the laboratory where holograms were made. As the film unfolded, I felt my secure, scientific view of nature slowly slipping away. An introduction to holography is a mind-boggling experience to almost anyone.

THE 3D EFFECT

First, we were shown a holographic recording of a statue of two horses pulling a chariot. After the holographic film had been developed there seemed to be no visible image on it when viewed in ordinary white light. Then it was exposed to the laser beam of light and all of a sudden the two horses and chariot came into view. They were located somewhere in space behind the holographic plate. As the plate was tilted from side to side, the images seemed to move, revealing different perspectives of the original sculpture. This ghost-like image could also be projected onto the laboratory wall.

Can you imagine my excitement at seeing this for the first time?

Next a cylindrical hologram was shown. Inside the cylinder was a white horse. It was photographed with laser light so that every visual angle of the statue would be recorded on the curved film. After the film was developed and the laser beam turned on, there in space was the horse suspended just as though it had never been taken away.

The cylinder was rotated, and the image of the horse rotated. Something that was no longer there was still rotating in front of my eyes.

Another sequence showed a small magnifying glass positioned in front of a little hand calculator. The two objects were recorded on holographic film. The objects were removed and the film was developed. When it was held up to the original laser beam, there was a non-existent magnifying glass magnifying a non-existent calculator. And, as it was moved, the glass magnified different parts of the calculator. Two objects that weren't there, were acting upon each other!

Then came a startling demonstration. The physicist had photographed two separate objects on one hologram plate; a small pony and a pair of dice. After the hologram was developed and projected on the screen I noticed something

peculiar. The laser light was a very narrow beam, and illuminated only a small portion of the plate, yet the entire picture was projected on the screen.

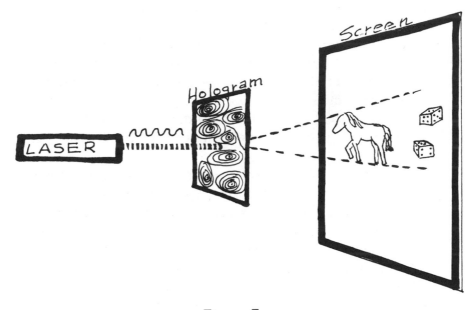

Figure 7

How could this be? Was the whole picture revealed no
matter what portion of the hologram was illuminated?

Then he did it! He took a hammer and broke the hologram
into pieces. "Well," I thought, "That ends the demonstration."

Wrong assumption. He took one tiny fragment from the
table and held it up to the laser light. There was the entire
picture of the pony and the dice. Nothing was missing.

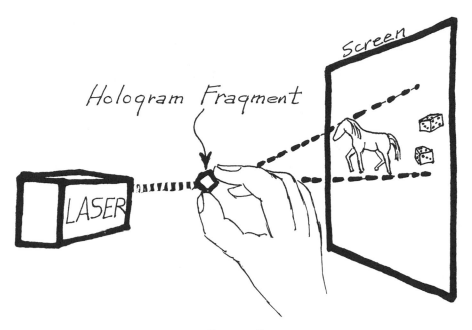

Figure 8

That was the moment that my mind made a quantum jump, and my universe turned upside down. EACH PART CONTAINED THE WHOLE.

I summarized what I had just seen of this phenomenon.

SEEING IS BELIEVING?

The image seen by looking through the hologram is 3D with both horizontal and vertical parallax.

The image appears to be located in space *behind a window*, (holographic plate.)

I could not distinguish the image from the actual object. They appeared identical.

The angle of viewing the image gives a unique perspective to the 3D image.

Each perspective is valid but at the same time is limited. To view the whole image one must be sure to view it from all perspectives, otherwise something may be hidden from view. (Figure 9)

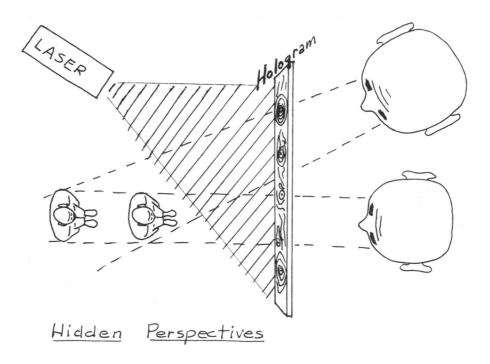

Hidden   Perspectives

Figure 9

Is there a contradiction in this statement? How can I say the hologram stores the whole picture everywhere if part of it may be blocked from view?

Objects which can be blocked from view are three dimensional. For example, in Figure 10 there are the words, "Whole Picture" on an ordinary photographic film. After the film has been developed, I will cut the photo into two pieces, leaving only the letter "E" to indicate the message. There is no way to tell what the rest of the word may be.

I can repeat that experiment using holographic film and a laser. After we have cut the hologram into two pieces as before, we notice the smaller piece still contains all the letters of "Whole Picture." Thus, a two dimensional object reveals the same picture from all perspectives.

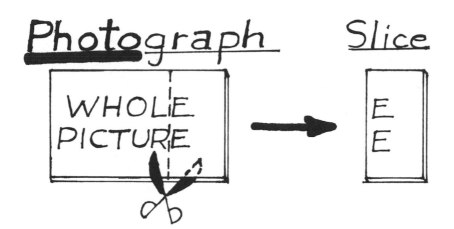

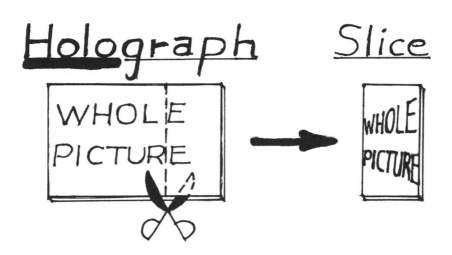

Figure 10

In addition to this phantom world behind the hologram there exists also an image out in front of it.

Projected   Image
Appearing in front of
Holographic   Plate

Figure 11

This image projected in front of the holographic plate is called "pseudoscopic" because it is turned inside out. The front of the wine glass is farthest back in space, and the back of the glass appears to be in front. It is a difficult image with which to work and can only be effectively seen by capturing it on a flat screen or making a second hologram from it. The second hologram again reverses the projected image. Only this time, it puts it back into its normal position.

HOW DOES HOLOGRAPHY WORK?

Holography is not a simple subject, and yet it will probably be regarded as one of the most important breakthroughs in our understanding since the beginning of science. You will be dealing with aspects of holography all through the rest of your life and it will be easier if you understand how it is created and what it can do.

For a good basic knowledge of the subject I recommend the book, *Understanding Holography* by Michael Wenyon, (Arco Publishing, 1978).

The basis of all photography is the light wave. Understanding how to record these waves, how they interfere with each other and how they can combine to create a record is our next venture. We will start by looking at the common wave.

THE WAVE

You may recall when you were a youngster that you were sitting at the edge of a still pond on a warm summer day. It was fun watching the reflection of the trees in the mirror-like surface. You asked yourself, "What would happen to the picture if I threw a rock in the water?"

That is what you did and the picture blurred and something more fascinating developed. That little stone began to generate a series of concentric waves, traveling out in all directions away from the disturbance.

Each wave left the point at the center as a perfect circle, expanding until its magnitude faded into the distance at the shore line. At first, the wave crest was high and its trough equally deep but as it expanded, this action diminished. That height is called the *amplitude*, or energy content, of the wave.

What we were observing was the universal phenomenon of WAVE PROPAGATION. Light does it. Sound does it. Atoms do it. Electrons do it. In fact any substance which can vibrate or radiate does it.

Every portion of the wave contains a certain perspective of

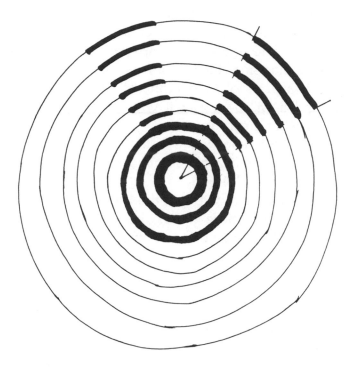

Radiation

Figure 12

the disturbance, radiating from the center—broadcasting from a point source. As the wave expands, it increases its breadth, but decreases its amplitude so consequently each point or section of the advancing wave contains a record of the original disturbance. Light is the perfect example of this process. It consists of electromagnetic waves.

Light propagates in a chain reaction. A fluctuating electric-field creates a fluctuating magnetic-field which create a fluctuating electric-field and so on at 186,000 miles per second. A point source of light acts like a pebble dropped into a pond, only now the waves travel vertically as well as horizontally.

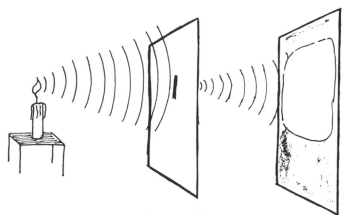

Figure 13

Above is a candle light passing through a thin slit in a piece of cardboard. As it passes through, light begins to radiate from the slit, all over again. We notice on the screen a broad circle of light, not just a thin line.

Now let us explore two such wave patterns intersecting in space.

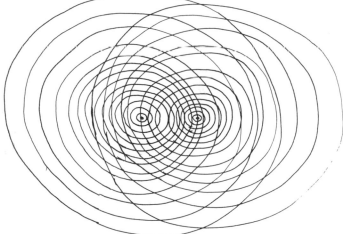

Figure 14a

We could create this interaction by putting a second slit in the original cardboard.

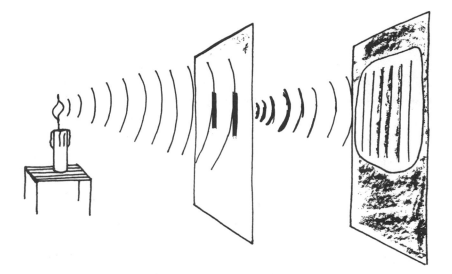

Figure 14b

As this light passes through the two slits, a strange thing happens on the screen upon which it is projected. A series of dark lines form on the screen. These lines represent the *phase* relationship between these two light waves. The spacing of these lines tells us how far apart the waves are and how pure their source is. Just the spacing alone reveals much about the relationship between the two waves.

Light waves interfering with other light waves can be frozen in space on a film and that is called a hologram.

It is becoming clear that this new type of photography is different in two areas. First, holography does not record an image on the film. Instead it records a pattern of light which is meaningless when seen under ordinary light. This meaningless pattern then creates the illusion of looking at an object through a window. Second, the holograph does not require a lens for focusing. The clarity of the holograph depends on the purity of light used. By purity of light I mean purity of color or frequency. This peculiar type of light can be found emanating from the laser, an artificial, man-made source of light.

WHY IS LASER LIGHT NECESSARY?

Light is an important factor because if you understand how light works and how you view your world, you will appreciate the relationship between illusion and reality a little more.

Do we really have to use a laser? What is so special about this kind of light? Why does the hologram owe its existence to this strange light source?

First, the laser produces light which has two characteristics uncommon to other types of light.

1. *Spatial Coherence, point source.* This means that all of the light generated by the laser appears to originate from a point, like dropping a pebble in a pond. Doesn't sunlight or lamp light have this characteristic? No, natural light appears to come from many points, not just one.

2. *Temporal Coherence, one frequency* (color). If you have ever seen a laser beam of light sparkling off of a dust particle in the air you have noticed its brilliant, pure color. No shades or tones of other colors are present. It is one vibrating color. Ordinary sunlight contains all colors which can be seen if it is separated by a prism. The deep red color is caused by a slower moving frequency than the higher rate of blue or violet. Laser light is fully coherent, both in space and time. This is essential in recording minute variations on the surface of an object being photographed. Such variations are compared to the unmodified Reference Beam and the phase difference is recorded in shades of dark and light on the photographic emulsion.

Making a holographic impression with white light (incoherent) results in blurs and rainbow-like streaking. Essentially it is out of focus and has no 3D properties. (There are some holograms that can be viewed with white light but they are created with coherent light.)

WHAT IS A LASER?

A laser is a device in which Light is Amplified through a gas or crystal to a high energy state. The device then Stimulates this excited light to release or Emit its energy through Radiation. Hence, the term "laser."

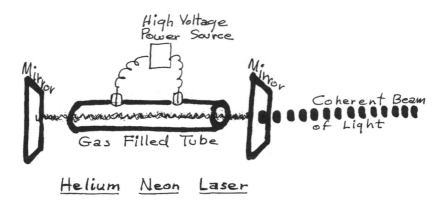

Figure 15

The gas filled tube is electrically excited to a high energy state. This light is then reflected back and forth between two mirrors. This builds a standing wave of light vibrating at one frequency. It is both spatially and temporally coherent.

The second of the two mirrors is only partially silvered and allows a small portion of light to pass right through. The escaping light is the popular laser beam used to create holograms, perform surgery on the eye, burn precision holes through steel and measure minute changes in the moon's orbit, among other things.

The power behind the laser may vary from one to two thousandths of a watt, used to photograph holograms, to tens of thousandths of watts used to burn holes through steel. The power behind the laser may vary but the principle remains the same—one of coherence.

(The mind also has the ability to acquire coherence although most of us go about, functioning in an incoherent world of our own making.)

MAKING A HOLOGRAM

Few of you intend to make holograms and may wonder what this has to do with you. The new perspectives that holography has made possible for us are as important, probably, as Galileo, Newton and Einstein gave us in their time. These new perspectives are a part of our era, and will become increasingly so. They carry us into the future. Most important are the insights they give to our manner of thinking and behavior. In later chapters you will see how the principles of holography apply to your whole life structure. When you understand how holograms are made you can make or remake the holographic patterns in your own mind that govern your life.

Go with me into a laboratory and let us watch a hologram being made.

We enter a dimly lighted room where we notice a table securely fastened to a stone foundation. We look for the source of soft red light that shines in the room. It comes from a laser mounted at the corner of the table. As we look closer we see that the shutter is closed so that no light is being projected onto the table. In the center of the table is our holographic film mounted in a secure fixture. On the front of the table is the object to be photographed, a small wine glass.

Everything is here—light, object, film, as in ordinary photography but how do we focus for this picture? Pictures

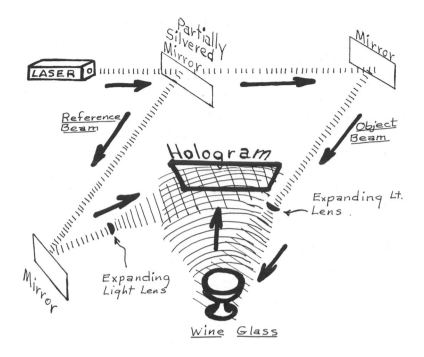

Figure 16

always have to be focused with a lens don't they? We find two lens offset from the hologram but these do not focus anything. They are there only to spread the laser light so it will illuminate the entire hologram and the object.

Looking more closely at the table we see two mirrors and a beam splitter. The beam splitter is a partially silvered mirror which allows a portion of the laser light to pass through it and the other part to reflect back off its surface.

"Quiet," someone says. "They're ready to take the picture."

We see the shutter open. A narrow beam of brilliant red light passes out of the tiny opening and strikes the beam splitter. The beam takes two paths. One leads to a mirror which reflects it over to the wine glass. The other strikes the mirror and onto the hologram plate. This holographic film now has two beams of light hitting its surface. (In ordinary photography that would create a double exposure or blurred image but this is a totally different process.) Both beams are necessary to record the variations in the surface of the object being photographed. One beam is called the "Object Beam," since it bounces off the wine glass. The other goes directly to the hologram plate and acts as a referent against which to measure the reflection of light off of the wine glass. It is called the "Reference Beam."

The laser light appears for only a little longer than the ordinary camera shutter would be opened. The technician sends the hologram plate out to be developed and when it is returned, it is mounted back in its holder.

At this point he removes the beam splitter and replaces it with a regular mirror. Only one beam is needed now. The wine glass has been removed. We are instructed to look through the hologram toward the spot where the glass had been on the table and there it is again—in three dimensions.

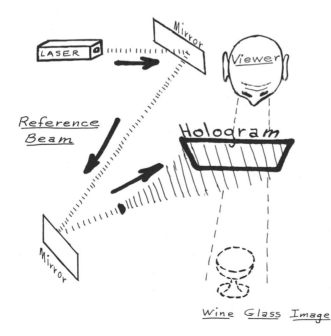

Figure 17

We look over the top and behind the plate but there is nothing there. The light in the laboratory is turned on and we can hold the plate up to that white light. It appears to have only some strange light and dark swirls, something like finger prints, on it. They are meaningless. They have no form or image in ordinary white light yet they have the potential to create a very real looking object in space when exposed to laser light. Where is the fine line between reality and illusion, and which is which?

WINDOW TO THE PAST

Think of the hologram as a window of time through which you can see into the past and examine an object which has long since been taken away. The window is also an excellent example of the whole picture being contained on a fragment.

Imagine standing outside of your house, looking into the living room through the front window. Everything is quite visible to you—furniture, lamps, carpeting, paintings on the walls, draperies, etc. Suppose we put masking tape over the window covering all but an inch square section of glass. By putting your eye up close to that hole, you can still look inside and see the sofa, chair, table and probably everything you saw in full vision. You don't see just one leg of a chair or one arm of a chair, do you?

Now, go to a corner of the window and peel back another piece of tape. As you look through that hole you can see everything in the room but from a different point of view. A chair may now block the view of a lamp, or the sofa a chair, but if you keep removing the tape you will be able to see the room from every angle, and everything in the room will be fully visible.

That is the effect one has when looking through a hologram. Each portion of the picture it contains has the whole imprinted on it but each fragment may limit the view to a certain perspective.

It is important to realize that by masking the window and leaving only one peep hole, I have fixed the perspective or attitude with which the whole room may be seen. This applies to our thinking process when we limit our perspective to one little opinion and insist that our viewpoint is the only true or right one.

HOLOGRAPHIC TIME

The hologram has been called a medium which transcends time. Why?

It is possible to photograph the past, present and future on a single plate. The unfolding of these time stages depends solely on the viewing angle. If you want to see the past, you hold the hologram at one angle. To see the future you shift the hologram to another angle. It is all there on one plate. Sounds confusing, doesn't it?

Let me illustrate this idea by using a clock.[1] We will photograph an ordinary clock on film with the laser process, except the reference beam will shine on the hologram from a specific angle for the first exposure. That exposure would record the clock hands at 7:01. The next exposure, on the same film, will take the clock hands at 7:02 with the reference beam at an angle shifted slightly from the first. The third exposure would be taken at 7:03 at yet another angle of the reference beam. On and on until we have exposed 1 hour of time in 1 minute increments on the same film.

When the plate has been developed, we can show the clock ticking in any number of ways. One is to move the hologram in the laser reference beam in exactly the same sequence in which it is filmed. The result would be to see the clock ticking off minute by minute in the sequential manner familiar to all of us.

Another method would be to allow the hologram to show the clock sequence up to 7:15, then quickly shift it to the angle of the laser beam at 7:29 and continue from there. This would give an apparent discontinuity. We would be jumping ahead in time and see the event happening before the prescribed interval. This would be "seeing the future" but since past, present and future are all recorded on the same hologram no matter how we view it, it is NOW.

Could the universe be constructed in this manner? Is that the secret of "everything is now"? (A term that has been so much used and so little understood.)

As we look into space with our powerful telescopes we find that we are looking farther and farther back into time. Yet, what is happening out there "now" won't be seen on this planet for another few thousand light years. In other words, "The *future* is happening right now in the *present* but will not be revealed to us until it has become part of the *past*."

So what is time? Is it another holographic illusion? Fortunately, most of us have agreed to see this illusion unfold sequentially. When you say, "I'll meet you at eight this evening," we both accept that a certain interval of time will pass before we actually meet.

This holographic view of time may help us understand those unusual people who seem to see ahead in time and predict with some degree of accuracy events which are going to occur. There have been prophets and mystics for ages and they are not loony or weird, just able to shift their laser beam of consciousness to illuminate the patterns of probabilities of things yet to appear.

Does this imply fatalism, pre-determination and that sort of nonsense?

No, it does not. The pattern of the universe, and in fact your pattern and mine can be *changed before* it is allowed to manifest. The universe is not made of concrete, nor is time. Heisenberg's uncertainty principle bears that out.[2] Patterns are pliable and can be molded at certain stages but once they have begun unfolding in time it is very difficult to change them. Understanding how this occurs is one of the purposes of this book.

APPLICATIONS OF HOLOGRAPHY

Holography has provided us a new window through which we may look out into another dimension and perceive

Reality in ways not possible before. Here are some of the areas which have been affected by this new science.

Computer Memories—Current research is under way to apply these techniques to enhance computer storage. There are several approaches; one uses a technique called the "flying spot,"in which a laser beam scans a holographic plate and illuminates the sector of desired information.

Information Storage—Another is condensing books. "It has been said that every book ever written could be put into a hologram approximately 5 × 5 inches square," stated Ed Bush, editor of *Holosphere*, in *Science Digest*.[3] We may be a few decades away from pouring all that knowledge into a 5 × 5 inch holographic plate, but it is a fact that we can record hundreds of separate pictures on a single holographic film and each picture will remain clear and distinct without double and multiple exposure occurring.

Banking Systems—"A French bank used a volume hologram memory system to store its clients' details. The 30 centimeter square plate was divided into many tiny volume holograms, each 2 millimeters square and each containing 60 holograms. This one foot square Holographic plate could store 60,000 pages of written information."[4]

(For a moment consider your memory device—the brain. Would nature design such an incredible storage system and not use the most efficient means available to it? That is unlikely. Apparently our memory operates on holographic principles.)

Medicine—The holographic principle has already been applied to the diagnostic methods. One uses radio frequencies to recreate a 3D image of internal organs for further examination without exploratory surgery or X-rays.[5]

Brain—The exciting new area of human memory research has been exploring the principles of holography to explain the memory process. Two excellent books on this subject are *Brain Shuffle* by Paul Pietsch and *Languages of the Brain* by Karl Pribram.

Philosophy—Dr. David Bohm, physicist at London University has proposed a fascinating new model of the universe based on holography. His book, *Wholeness and the Implicate Order*, is an open door to a new understanding of reality and consciousness.

Psychology—New methods of mental images and human consciousness are being described in holographic terms. It has been given a new understanding of how the subconscious mind makes and holds impressions and, using the principles of holography, how they can be dealt with more quickly and efficiently.

Parapsychology—New answers for old questions are becoming available through understanding the mysterious areas of phenomena such as "remote viewing", ESP, ghosts, out-of-body and near-death experiences.[6]

Art—New forms of 3D art have been introduced. The Museum of Holography in New York City has one of the largest collections of this type of art. Priceless treasures could be holographically reproduced on cylindrical plates and shipped anywhere without endangering the originals. An Amerindian child in Arizona or Montana may see the magnificent "David," in full detail as Michelangelo carved him, in his little school room. The crown jewels could be reproduced in full, glowing colors, and examined by visitors in cities around the world, without any fear of theft or damage.

Entertainment—Movies such as "Logan's Run" used holography displays for special effects. Disney Land in Anaheim uses holographic displays to fool the observer as he or she rides through the famous haunted house. There are ambitious attempts being made to produce holographic programs for TV viewers so that the football game will appear projected right into the living room and the viewers may feel they can get into the play. Violent scenes of shootings and bloody conflicts, screeching tire car chases and scary encounters may be seen in what appears to be reality around you—without making you clean up the messes.

Think of a hologram projected into your livingroom of a cool, shaded forest, miles from city noises or stress. With added sounds of flowing streams and bird songs, you could have a mini-vacation without leaving home.

The possibilities are endless. There is hardly a field which has not received some impact from this new "Whole Picture" discovery. Most of all it is changing our lives from what now appears to be more of an old flat-earth concept to infinite wholeness and interrelatedness. We can no longer run and hide and be separate. The thoughts we think, the feelings we have, the words that we speak go out like ripples in the pond.

MIND AS IMAGE MAKER

"The Mind is Slayer of the Real"

— The Vedas

4 To say that we live in an image world may be startling but consider that everything that has been made by the human was first an image in his mind. And, if in some cases something was made by accident, his imagination found a way to use it.

The ability to image-make (imagine) separates us from the animals. So far as we know no animal can imagine something and then bring it into being. If a beaver builds a dam or a bower bird a nest, it is from instinct or observation. Only the human can let an image form in some part of his brain and hold it before his "mind's eye" until he has duplicated that image into form—whether it is a toothpick or a rocket, a magnificent painting or a giant bridge. So, the image-making ability is a creative process that makes us unique among all other forms of life on this planet.

Mind has the ability to create images not unlike those seen behind and in front of the holographic plate. It does this while we are awake or dreaming. Where do these 3D images come from? Why are they so real that in some instances, as in nightmares, they cause us to awaken crying out in fear, with mouth dry and heart palpitating?

Even when there is no sensory stimulation from the surrounding environment, such as I experienced in the sensory-deprivation tank, I found that the mind brought up myriads of pictures. Real as those images appeared to be I knew that they were only illusions whose roots could be traced back to some past registry of the senses. This sort of mind-dancing goes on most of the time in our heads, causing us to over-lay past images, or future imaginings, on the present. Some of them are pleasant, and some so startling or frightening that they result in traumas and phobias. Frequently these images from the past prevent us from giving our full attention to the present.

Holography presents a possible answer to how the mind forms images. THE BRAIN MAY BE HOLOGRAPHIC IN ITS STRUCTURE. This seems far-fetched but it could be nearer the truth than any other approach to understanding the phenomena of thinking, remembering, dreaming and imagining.

Dr. Karl Pribram, neuro-psychologist, presents some interesting data from his research to support his idea. His theory of a holographic memory was published in *Scientific American* in 1969.[1] He elaborated on the theory in his text, *Languages of the Brain* in 1971.[2] Since then articles about it have appeared in *Human Behavior Magazine*,[3] *Psychology Today*,[4] and *Omni*[5] among others.

MEMORY

Memory, that elusive function of the brain appears not to be stored in discrete compartments but is spread, or distributed, over wide areas of the cortex. It is not possible to surgically remove your memory of your first day at school, although it may be reduced to a dim recall. In amnesia and comatose states, the memories apparently lie there even if they can not be stimulated to recognition by a conscious state at a given time.

Shortly after Dr. Pribam's theory had been published, Dr. Paul Pietsch, anatomist at Indiana University, put the theory to the test. Using salamanders, he performed hundreds of brain transplants in search of memory engrams. He ended up being a proponent of the Pribram theory and wrote a delightful book, describing his explorations, titled, *Shuffle-Brain, the Quest for the Hologramic Mind.*

If these men are on the right track, and their data is very convincing and credible, then the question arises, "Where is the laser in my head?" (A hologram depends on coherent light, remember?) The laser counterpart may be no more than my focus of attention.

Dr. Pribram speculates that these holographic images are formed through a combined wave front involving the *Frontal Lobes* (attention-focusing part of the brain) and the *Limbic System* (feeling-emotion area of the brain.) The more intense one feels about an experience the more vivid the recall will be.

You may remember sitting through a dull lecture, seeing and thinking of things miles away but when the professor said, "This question will be on the final exam," you came to the present with strict attention. It is similar to taking a picture of a distant mountain when suddenly a bee lights on the finger that is ready to press the camera button. The mind forgets the mountain, and sees only the bee—close up!

The thinking process resembles the laser procedure in many ways. Sometimes it is tuned and coherent, at other times it is incoherent. To re-create an experience from the past we must first put full attention on the memory. That attention may be guided consciously or drift unconsciously, but something has to trigger the previous experience like turning a camera on a screen, then the mind re-runs an old episode. Frequently, this is brought out by a sensory stimulation, a sight, sound or smell can awaken an entire sequence.

ASSOCIATION

As an example—suppose I am driving down the freeway on my way to work, feeling good about myself and the world, and out of the corner of my eye I catch a glimpse of the girl in a car next to mine. She looks like Rachel. I glance over and realize that she is not Rachel but the resemblance sets off a chain of memories and feelings of the time that I dated her. I am seeing them, re-living them, when suddenly I am aware that while I was driving and my physical sight was fastened to guiding my car through rush hour traffic, I missed my turn off. Now I have to drive miles to the next exit and I'll be late for work and the entire day will be set to a discordant tempo. I am so irritated (at myself, really) that I decide everyone else is a stupid driver, trying to crowd me out; I am a victim of illusions. Actually, it all resulted from my having chosen to give more importance to a holographic image than to what I was doing at the time.

Another instance can be, you may be sitting in your living room, content with your life and your mate. It is a good life that you have together, nothing lacking—then from the radio comes an old song that was "our song" in some earlier romance. Your mind drags you back through that, and you wonder what life would have been if you had married the other person. You look at your mate now with a different attitude. Comparison comes, and a sense of displeasure, which may erupt into a quarrel. A very real quarrel fostered by pure illusion.

Or, you may be walking along, enjoying a beautiful autumn day and as you pass a house with opened doors, a whiff of pickling spices reaches your nostrils and there you are, back in grandmother's kitchen while she is canning. She made so many delicious things, cookies and pies—and she loved you and spoiled you, and now that she is gone you feel forsaken and lonely and the world is dreary. Suddenly you are in a miserable mood and the day is clouded.

Happy memories may be brought about in this manner, also. Driving past a campus you see the capped and gowned graduates hurrying along to the ceremonies and your heart quickens, remembering the day you graduated. How proud you were and how successful you had felt. Your shoulders straighten and you breathe more deeply. You are young and filled with hope again.

WORRY

Worry is another example of looking through old holograms. We deliberately call up frightening images from the past—and project them into the future. It goes something like this: I am scheduled to give a sales pitch for the company tomorrow. I feel uncertain and unprepared. There wasn't time to do all the research that needed to be done. What if I can't answer all of the questions satisfactorily? I'll be letting the company down. It happened once before and I was so embarrassed I wanted to quit the job and disappear. If that happens again, I'll lose my job and the car payment is due. It isn't fair. They expect too much of me and don't give me the help I need. It's their fault if I fail. Why should I beat my brains out for a corporation that knows me only by a number—takes my life in, chews it up and spits it out. I'm expendable. But—the car payment is due and I have a pain in my stomach which is probably an ulcer, and I don't have medical insurance—and on and on.

Such imaging, associated with feeling, can cause physical illness besides depression, loss of a job, and a host of other negative effects, all resulting from the mind creating pictures of illusions!

PROJECTED HOLOGRAMS

Some people are so emotionally intense that they project an image from their past onto other people they meet. It is hard for them to get to know you because they can't see YOU. They see only their projection of what they think you are. The first time you meet someone like this he informs you, "You remind me of my uncle Harry. He had red hair just like you and a temper. I'll bet you've got a temper to match. You even talk like him." That person sees you through Uncle Harry's hologram and expects you to behave as Uncle Harry and if you don't he will decide that you are trying to deceive him. This happens so often in marriage. The man or woman projects the image of his or her ideal on their mate and is blinded to what that person really is as a person. When they arrive at the marriage counselor, the label placed on the problem is "lack of communication." They have never communicated with one another. The ideal mate that they thought they had married never existed outside of their minds. It was another illusion.

DREAMS

In the dream state there are incredibly real holographic images we relate to every night. Dr. Carl Jung considered them to originate largely from the Collective Unconscious. This could be nothing more than a subconscious holographic domain that we deposit into, and draw out from, jointly. Certainly the dream world appears real and most of the time we do not recognize it as a dream while it is happening. The subconscious plays a significant role in determining the content of the dream state, however. Most of the time it can be traced back to some sense perception which the brain has received in the past twenty-four hours, according to Dr. Nagendra Das, in his research in sleep and dreams, at University of Michigan. He concluded that the brain registered masses of sensory stimulation, much of it outside of conscious awareness, and if it could not release this in the dream state, it would "explode" in some type of neurosis. (Other research has determined that people deprived of dreaming, for only a few nights, begin to hallucinate and may go into serious derangement.) This nightly replay does not apply to the more rare cases of recurring dreams which can be meaningful, or those dreams that present themselves with symbolic significance when the dreamer expects that. The subconscious will comply with expectation, no matter how ridiculous it appears.

EXPECTATION

Expectation is an important key in understanding how these mind-holograms are created. Some people are so terrified by the world "out there" that they create worse worlds in their minds as self protection. That is, they expect the worst in order not to be disappointed. They think that prepares them for the disasters that are sure to come. They do not guess that they are creating that worst by their expectation! This type of reverse anticipation may buffer the occurence of phobias but it is an insult to life to so misdirect it.

POWER OF IMAGES

Images formed by the mind can be so powerful that they can actually cause death. There is a much told story of an Indian boy who ran into the family's hut, screaming that a poisonous snake had bitten him. Blood dripped from the punctured skin on his leg. The terror was so great that it caused his heart to stop and he died. The next morning his family went up the path where he had been attacked and there was a piece of rope lying next to a thorn bush. He had seen the rope, which his mind interpreted to be a snake, and he had felt the stab from the thorn as he jumped aside and his mind supplied the image of the snake bite. Illlusion had killed the boy.

This illustrates the danger of assigning false values to these images.

If we reverse this process, we find we can actually change our reality through the conscious use of mental images. Dr. Carl Simonton, and his wife, Stephanie, have shown this in so many instances of treating cancer at their clinic.

Most successful people refer to an essential ingredient in their success as the ability to have a clear image of what they desire and to hold it. They do not let it fade but support it with enthusiasm and confidence.

If it is really all that simple why aren't more people successful? They fail because so many people have emotionally charged images from the past that are superimposed onto the present. These past images create conflicts and interrupt the creative imagery procedure.

In the next chapter we will explain the techniques for dealing with these troublesome images from the past.

PSYCHOLOGICAL HOLOGRAMS

All Psychological Pain is the Result of Buying into an Illusion.

5 We have been proposing a model for the brain and mind which differs radically from the usual models. First the holographic model allows the mind to work outside of time.

Since time is relative to the observer, each of us must be involved in creating our own perception of time. Where the old techniques of therapy relied on time as a healer, the holographic model allows the person to determine his own duration for healing. This is understandable when you realize that the past, present and future all exist simultaneously in the hologram. We can choose how we shall experience a sequence of events.

As we mentioned before—when you look up at the stars, you are looking backwards, perhaps millions of light years, into the PAST. Stars that may be dying or exploding NOW will not be seen here until some time in the FUTURE. So, the future, which is ocurring in the now, can be seen only in the past.

It is clear how these three aspects of time exist together. We only view them as separate, and any view we take is valid for us at that moment. If we don't like one aspect we can shift to see it from another perspective.

Second, the hologram shows us the process for creating and *changing images in time.*

Many people have expressed a wish to go back in time and change their response to an event or situation. They were told, "Of course, you can't change the past!" The principles of holography disagree with that statement.

A picture, or image, coded with a feeling, holds the simple ingredients needed to record a psychological hologram. The accompanying illustration gives an idea of how this works.

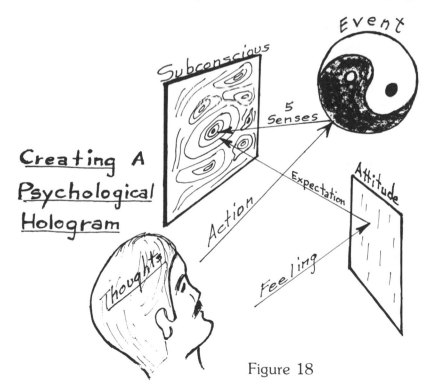

Figure 18

The thought process in many ways resembles the laser. It can be tuned to a single, very pure frequency or feeling, with which to view a hologram out of the past. That is done by seeing-feeling the incident recurring.

In the figure THOUGHT can act as the laser source of both *action* and *feeling*. These two coherent waves are essential for the first step in making a psychological hologram on the subconscious "plate." Feeling is like a tone in sound, or a color in light. It can be very coherent. As a pure feeling it is directed by the *attitude* mirror and is reflected in *expectation*. (We usually expect something to happen in a certain way. Seldom does it turn out just as we expected. If it does we may have created a positive impression and have a happy memory. When it doesn't and if we are deeply disappointed or frightened, we have made a negative holographic impression. Phobias are typical of the latter.)

Consider next, the *action* wave. It produces a "happening" to which our senses respond, triggering an impression in the brain. The Interference pattern between the expectation and actual occurrence stamps the imprint on the subconscious, making a psychological hologram. The stronger the feeling about the experience the more intensely the image is recorded. Over the years we record innumerable impressions in this manner.

RECREATING THE IMAGE

In order to view such a hologram we must first put attention on the pattern, then the image will take on the appearance of reality. (One does not see the picture in the holographic film until a light of a certain frequency is shown upon it, so in the subconscious, the image does not become visible until we have activated it with a certain thought-feeling.) This may be done consciously or unconsciously, often stimulated by sensory association. The unconscious process involves permitting the senses to free-wheel or drift with whatever captures their attention. The conscious process involves directing the attention through guided imagery.

However, to achieve success in this, the mind must first be brought into a very coherent state. This is done easily by using autogenic relaxation techniques. Once the brain enters the alpha state (approximately seven to thirteen cycles per second) the mind slips into idle picturing. It is as though you began to page through a series of past holograms, using a brilliant, high intensity laser. Many of these holographic images in our past contain trapped energy which must be released before we can realize a happy and wholesome life.

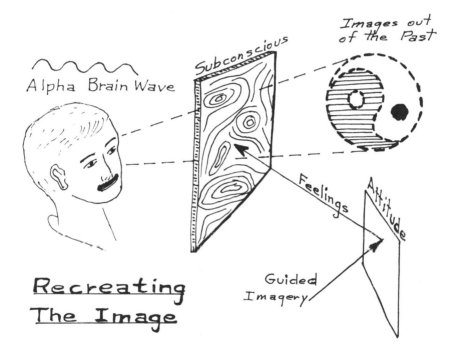

Figure 19

We can not explain just how the subconscious chooses to select specific traumatic incidents out of the multitudes of memories, but it may be by the suggestion given to seek it out.

DEALING WITH PSYCHOLOGICAL HOLOGRAMS

There are basically three ways to deal with any psychological hologram:

1. Change of attitude or perspective.
2. Change of feeling.
3. Replace it with a new memory.

Examples of these techniques, applied psychologically, will be given further on.

In this diagram you will see how an attitude toward an event can be changed by simply shifting the perspective. To look at the whole picture instead of one aspect of it, or evaluate the event from another person's viewpoint.

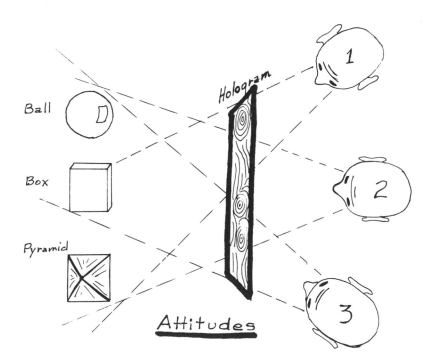

Figure 20

CHANGE OF ATTITUDE

Each of these persons is viewing the same hologram that contains three objects; a ball, a box, and a pyramid. The person in the middle can see all three. The one in the upper corner has the ball cut from his vision and sees only the box and pyramid and the one in the lower corner can not see the pyramid but only the box and ball.

Wars have been fought, lives lost, divisions caused in religions and social groups, and governments toppled over so small a thing as someone refusing to change his view point. To say to the first man, "There is also a ball on that hologram," is futile because he can't see it. Neither can the third man see the pyramid. Each is right in his belief of what he sees, from his viewpoint. Unless he can be moved to see the larger picture, he will be willing to die for what he believes to be true. He may not suffer physical death, but holding to a limited viewpoint or conviction in his emotional world can be a type of death—at least a self-inflicted imprisonment.

CHANGE OF FEELING

This process differs from the previous one in that one can observe the situation from the same point of view and still cause a shift in perception.

Using the box again as an example: The box is a pattern of dark lines on white paper. In my imagination, I create the image of a box from the pattern of lines. Not only does the box come to life, but I can cause it to move in and out, forming two different appearances. I do this, not by moving my head from side to side, but by shifting my *feeling* about the box.

If I feel strongly enough about the lower face of the box being forward, it will come forward. Conversely, if I feel strongly that the upper face of the box is forward, it will move forward in my mind.

In the same way we can view an experience in life as detrimental and frightening, and it will certainly appear to be just that. However, within that same experience is an opportunity, as a new beginning, whose other perspective is

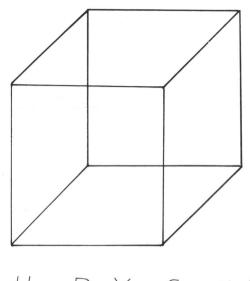

How Do You See it ?

Figure 21

waiting to be revealed by a shift in our feeling.

When the feeling is strong enough, the box shifts—and a whole new perspective comes into existence—in our mind. (Nothing "out there" changes.) But, you may say, "The box seems to shift on its own without my changing my feeling about it." If that happens, it can give you a feeling of insecurity and helplessness, of being a victim. The important thing to realize here is that you have a choice as to how you will see the box. Exercise that choice. Don't let the box "do it to you." Determine to see it one way, and then will to see it the other way. The appearance will obey your will.

REPLACEMENT

You will remember that in a previous chapter I mentioned the volume hologram and how hundreds of different pictures could be printed on a single photochromic crystal by changing the angle of the film with respect to the reference beam. What allowed each picture to be separate and distinct was that each one was recorded at a slightly different angle. Each picture could be caused to reappear by using the same reference beam at that particular angle.

If a phobia has a holographic origin then it could be changed as quickly as it was impressed. All that is required is to bring up the same picture-experience, (memory) and its associated feeling. Once that is done it is like being in a laboratory, ready to take another exposure on the original holographic film. This second exposure is the person's re-creation of the past in which the outcome has a satisfactory result—the way the person would liked to have it happen.

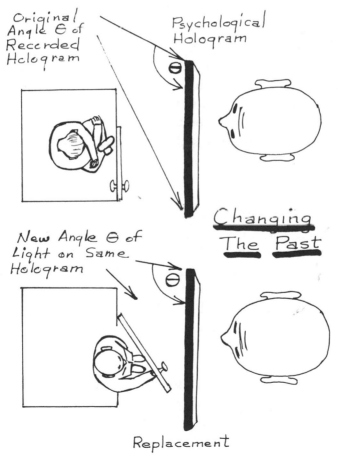

Figure 22

EXAMPLE

John is 45 years old and has had claustrophobia as early as he can remember. He is now guided into a state of relaxation, using autogenic techniques, (visual imagery and soothing music) until he is seeing his past clearly. This is similar to tuning the laser. After he has felt comfortable in passing through pleasant past experiences, the important question is asked.

"When was the first time you felt trapped and enclosed in a confined area? Let your mind show you the incident." (It is important to suggest, "show" because we want to deal with the right hemisphere where picturization dominates instead of verbalization.)

John feels himself to be a little boy, about four years old, locked in a dark closet in his home. He is terrified and begins to cry. (The emotional component is necessary.) He describes the situation in detail. He had disobeyed his father **and unlocked the gate and run away with some neighbor** children. His father had locked him in the closet in order to teach him a lesson. The lesson he learned was—to stay out of closed areas!

Can this experience be changed? We remind John that he is much smarter now, even though he sees himself locked in the closet. He is told to feel around in the closet and find something to stand on. He finds a piece of luggage, pulls it over to the door and stands on it. He is now tall enough to reach the knob. Actually, he finds, the door wasn't locked **and as he turns the knob, the door opens.**

"What are you going to do now?" he is asked.

"I'm going to run out!"

"How does it feel?"

"It feels so good to get out of that dark, scary place."

At this point a new holographic impression has been imprinted on his subconscious mind. He has visualized and emotionally experienced it. He has felt it, and the relief of being free.

Will so simple a procedure last? Yes, if John wants it to.

Both holograms are there. He has a choice of which one he wishes to focus upon. The next time he enters an elevator and the old habit pattern of fear begins to close in, he has only to remember that he walked out of that closet by his own effort and recall the sense of freedom that he felt. He has control of the situation.

This is a way that one may "change the past" to suit one's needs. If you feel that you were deprived and unloved as a child, try this technique—relax with soft, restful music and let your imagination give you the childhood that you wish you had known; devoted, loving parents who believed in you and helped you bring out your talents, who were proud of your smallest accomplishment and who were always there to encourage you, even if you had failed. FEEL it so intensely that when your mind brings you back to "now" you will retain that confidence as a new part of your being.

"But," someone will disagree. "That's fantasy. That can be dangerous."

"Aren't the unhappy memories you harbor more dangerous? Especially when you are letting them influence, even dominate, much of your living."

In order to arrive at this replacement state of a psychological hologram, the person needs to meet certain conditions.

—The person must have a real desire, and belief, that he or she can change it.

—The person must be able to relax and go into an alpha state of mind.

—The person must be free from apprehension about encountering the old experience.

—The person must expect to feel the desired experience with the same intensity as the previous frightening memory held.

—The person must realize that MEMORY and IMAGINATION are made of the same substance. One is no more "real" than the other. Both deal with illusions. If you do not agree with this, the next time you are very hungry, try satisfying your hunger with the memory of last Thanksgiving Day's feast. You will be convinced of its unreality.

It is essential that you detach yourself from the illusions of thinking that you are your mind. Identify with the Observer, the Real You, who can use the mind as a tool.

HOLOGRAPHY and PSYCHOLOGY

(The application in therapy)

—*Laurel Elizabeth Keyes*

When I studied pyschology I was sure that it was the answer to whatever problems people might have. It did not interest me because of personal problems. I had enjoyed a happy childhood, was much loved, and growing up in ranch country in the West where plains were broad and mountains high, I could observe natural forces in all forms of life.

But, for people in cities, out of touch with nature, the study of the mind and how to explore it and work with it seemed to offer a wonderful way to help troubled ones to live more balanced and satisfying lives.

A fine, old doctor friend had remarked one day, as he watched a patient leave his office, "If I could bottle love and prescribe it, I could cure all of the ills in the world." Since that was not possible, the next best thing must be to understand the way the mind dominated lives in success or failure, misery or contentment and health or illness.

Psychology was a vast new world that opened up unlimited possibilities. I was as dedicated to it as one might be to a religious concept. I believed it could cure anything. It was the only tool necessary.

Along with my studies, I worked for some psychiatrists. I watched their patients go through long and expensive treatment. I copied case histories and saw so little progress that I became disillusioned. So much time was spent analyzing the cause of a problem that little was left to attend to the healing. It was like seeing a person come in with a splinter in his foot that pained him every time he walked. He would be asked, "Where did you get the splinter?"

He would answer, "I don't know. I guess I stepped on some wood somewhere."

"What kind of wood?"

"Why, from a tree I suppose."

"What kind of a tree? Where did it grow? How tall was it? On rocky soil or fertile? Was it a dead tree or alive? How long had it been dead?" and on and on about the tree, and little about the foot or the person attached to the foot. It seemed to me that all that was needed was to take the splinter out and discard it. If the therapist were proficient, he should be able to do that rather quickly and with little expense.

Nature had taught me that if one buries a skunk, the earth will convert it into some new growth, perhaps a flower. If one returns to dig up the carcass time after time, nothing new will grow from it, no change will occur, and it remains a stinking mess. My logic asked if a trauma could be caused in one incident, sometimes in a few seconds, why did it require years of digging at it to try to correct it?

Happily, years later, Prigogine's theory of Dissipative Structures substantiated my conviction that such help as guided imagery could result in the "sudden relief of a lifelong phobia or ailment. An individual reliving a traumatic incident in a state of highly-focused inward attention perturbs the pattern of that specific old memory. This triggers a reorganization—a new dissipative structure.[2] The old pattern is broken."

Over the years I had investigated many of the fringe therapies—the "ologies" and group sessions and exploratory types of experiences. Most could be placed in two categories: 1) Encouraging the person to "be yourself," without making clear what that self was to become. Usually this self referred to the indulgent and immature persona or mask-self which refused to take any responsibility for one's state, but looked for someone (often parents) to blame. 2) Demanding that people reshape their lives beyond their natural capacity. The methods were brutal and often, harmful.

The one thing these methods seemed to have in common was enormous fees for the small amount of benefit that resulted.

I could not determine marked improvement in the lives of people who participated in these therapies. There were changes but these changes gave the appearance of making the person seem more self-centered, inconsiderate of others and controlled by certain identifiable patterns of behavior and vernacular—as well as dependent upon the treatment or group relationships. They seemed to have traded one set of boundaries for another without questioning. The methods did not bring the people to an unselfish, confident and joyous attitude that I would regard normal and wholesome.

In the group work people talked a great deal about love and there was much hugging and physical contact but there was little evidence of compassion and consideration for people outside of their own groups. Their therapies seemed to have restricted them inward to self-interest instead of extending them into a larger world of free embracement of all people and all life.

A few of the more aggressive ones found reinforcement for their attitudes and behavior. They were assured that it was natural to be angry, and express it, regardless of whom it might harm. (There was no indication that they could learn *not to become* angry in the first place and so have more control over their impulses, encouraging more humanism and less animality in their expressions.) These therapies urged them to "do their own thing," focusing on infantile "me-oriented" viewpoints instead of attempting to mature in more responsible and civilized directions.

The sensitive people were the casualties—in group sessions or in association with aggressive persons, in family or working relationships. I witnessed one such result of a confrontation type therapy. A gentle woman became a target for the group who insisted that she was with-holding hostilities and was pretending to be "good and sweet." Members of the group taunted her, ridiculed her, slapped her and did everything they could to make her angry and behave as *they thought* she should. Instead she became hysterical, after which they forced her to consume whiskey (which she had never before drunk) to relax her. Consequently, her kidneys stopped functioning. For the rest of that week, for which she had committed herself, and paid, she had to wear a catheter. When she returned to her home, it was necessary for her to undergo major surgery to repair the damage from that traumatic so-called therapy experience. And, that technique was one used by the oldest and best-known group therapy institutions. (It is still being used with variation, some milder and others even more violent.) Since then we have accounts of people who have had to go to mental hospitals, and some have lost their lives while participating in such mind-changing groups, experiencial confrontations supposed to assist people in "finding themselves."

Verbal assaults that strip away self-worth, dignity and ideals can be as deadly as ripping open an abdomen and leaving the contents spilling out, expecting the patient to put everything back together and heal himself, if he can. Many can not. I have known some high school students who had undergone such practices and lost all confidence in themselves, and incentive to continue their schooling. I have witnessed numerous divorces resulting from this type of encountering. So much negative physical and emotional reaction can not be in harmony with natures' principles which created the marvelous and complex system of the human body and brain. How could a treatment be successful that dealt with this miracle as though it were a machine of metal, or stone to be broken and reshaped? There had to be a better method, I insisted.

During my years of counseling I used methods that were compatible with the natural unfolding processes found in nature, especially in the seed. The results were gratifying. When I discovered Toning, I felt that was a way of working with the very basic nature of the whole person. Results were remarkable in both physical healings and mental attitudes.

(Those are reported in my book, *Toning, Creative Power of the Voice*.) But, I did not know exactly how or why healings followed. Dr. William Tiller, at Stanford, gave me some indication in his theory of "Negative Space Time" but I needed more understanding of it.

I knew there was more than just faith involved because in some instances people who were helped did not know Toning had been directed toward them. However, faith was a factor in healing that could not be ignored. I had been present at many faith healings in religious services, such as Oral Robert's and Kathryn Khulman's and other evangelists. I had seen people put aside crutches and wheel chairs, and walk. Some of my friends had been healed of diabetes and twisted limbs. The puzzling thing was that not all of the sincere, believing and praying audience received healings. Surely, all had faith or they would not have been there. Out of three thousand, I saw perhaps eighty who had correction of their ailments and not all of them would keep their healings. When they returned home someone might insist, "That's impossible. You know the doctors have said you couldn't be cured. You were just hypnotized." And, they would return to their old conditions. Why? If they had walked without help, why couldn't they continue?

I could not accept the idea that a just and loving God could be so capricious as to heal some and ignore the desperate pleas of others. Religion could give me no satisfactory answer.

It appeared that these healings were triggered in some part of the brain below the cortical functioning. They were associated, as far as I could determine, with emotional fervor in the individual or in an audience charged with intense expressions of sound and feelings. There must be some vibratory action that penetrated the limbic system of the brain; the old mamillian brain was impelled to accept a different pattern. Perhaps all healing was instantaneous (like the image of the box shifting) but permanence depended upon keeping that focus (or feeling) on the new condition instead of the former conviction of illness.

Healing did not depend on the instrument through which it came as much as on RELEASING a quality in the patient. It didn't seem to matter whether this was done by a Christian evangelist, an Amerindian medicine man, an African witch doctor, faith healer or counselor. *Something in the patient's brain caused the body to accept a change.*

For those who insist that unless a healing is done in the name of a certain religion it is not done by God, but by the devil, I believe that all healing must come only from the great Creative Process, "God," because if correction of ills could be done by any evil, or form of negativity, that would soon put itself out of business wouldn't it? Evil, like a shadow, has no power of its own. Only when we give it power can it manifest.

The sun shines through many windows. Some are large, some small. Some are dirty, some clean, some are of stained glass, some are broken, and they limit the light according to their size and state but the light that comes through them is from the one sun, ("one God").

Normalcy, health and happiness are in the realm of harmony and beauty—as flowers blossom and the stars keep in their orbits. What we call "good" is evidence of balance and peace and adheres to a given pattern upon which it was formed originally. (Some people refer to this idea as "God's Will.") It is there for anyone who finds a way to accept and use it. Healing, whether of mind or body, must follow the same principle—IDENTITY WITH, AND ACCEPTANCE OF ITS NATURAL PATTERN.

The question was, "How to accomplish this in dependable and certain ways?"

When I was first introduced to holography my mind took a quantum leap. This was something that made sense! It explained to me how the subconscious mind accepted incidents and created a reality that appeared to be substantive; to be so real that the entire mind structure was influenced by the illusion. This was how healings appeared. And, if that was how traumas and blockages were created, then the PRINCIPLES OF HOLOGRAPHY COULD BE APPLIED FOR CORRECTION OF THEM.

Finally, I had an answer to so many questions.

I discussed my ideas with Paul, since he had a good understanding of holography. He was cautious about accepting my hypothesis but when I began using it and he saw the results, he agreed, "This is in keeping with holographic principles."

Through holographic concepts he began studying the brain from new viewpoints. He had been in an area of probing outer space but this inner space was far more exciting.

That old adage, "If you *think* you are well but *feel* ill, you will remain ill. If you *feel* well, you are well," was understandable to me in terms of cortical functioning, and the powerful influence of the limbic system of the brain. Talking and reasoning did not always get back to the seat of emotions where the conviction had been rooted. The emotions had to be engaged to cause the "box to shift" and allow another way of seeing the situation. And, for permanent help, the new perspective had to be maintained or the old way of seeing it would appear to be real again. (The problem would return to the old viewpoint.)

Now I could put faith healings in two categories. Those rare instances in which there was an instant and complete healing, (The persons were convinced in a fraction of a second when their minds shifted to acceptance.) And, the more common ones in which the person saw the healing as possible, (again, a new conviction) but accepted it on faith before there was evidence of it. The total healing may not be manifested for months but during that period faith had to support the conviction; the new way of seeing the "shifted" condition.

In the natural order of things I could associate it with the conception of a child. A child is conceived in a moment. In that moment it is a potential human but it is not formed as a normal human for nine months. There has to be an incubation period in which that child is nourished, and protected while it forms on its inherent pattern. At no time is it not a *potential* human and probably little time in which the mother's body is not aware of the change and growth going on inside of it.

In the case of healing, the moment that the feeling of perfect health is accepted back there in the deep part of the brain, the "box shifts" (not a slow turning but instantaneously) and there is a conception, a union of potential formation and the body's natural pattern. That new conviction must be held unerringly. If doubt or despair enter the person's mind before the healthy formation is completed, the healing will be aborted. And the person must start all over again with another "conception" experience.

I heard a woman tell of her experience of being blinded for twelve years as the result of a car accident. During an intense prayer and spiritual experience, sight returned to her in an instant. She could read a newspaper held up for her. She saw her husband and child for the first time. Elated, she returned to her doctor to show him the miracle. After careful examination the doctor shook his head.

"Your eyes are not healed," he said. "They are just the way they were. You are still blind."

"But I can see you," she persisted, describing him, the clothes that he wore, and reading the charts on the wall.

"I don't know what you're seeing with but it can't be your eyes," he insisted sadly.

This did not shake the woman's conviction. She retained her ability to see.

Now, I could understand this. As you read in earlier chapters, the eye by itself does not see, the brain does. But what caused that brain to see when others could not, is still one of the mysteries that we have not yet solved. If something happens back there in its depths, apparently some deep emotion that touches the limbic system, the brain is convinced that it can see—and it sees; that legs can walk and they walk. Some frequency, light, sound or emotion sets off a natural law to reinstate its pattern.

We know that salamanders can regrow a member or tail when one has been severed. And, electrical stimulation to a leg stub of a rat caused the leg to extend, growing almost to its original length. Fingers and hands of humans have been known to be rejoined, and function again.

Apparently AS LONG AS THE PATTERN REMAINS VITAL, Life will accumulate substance around it. This proves that the PATTERN IS THE REALITY, not the formation . (Does this explain that familiar verse, "Faith is the substance of things hoped for."?) One may have a pattern, as for a chair. The chair can be burned but as long as the pattern is in someone's mind other chairs may be made from it. That which is transitory is the illusion. If we learn nothing more from holography than that—we have made a giant step forward in our evolutionary plan, to see the real beyond the illusion.

Before giving examples of using holographic principles, I would like to answer some questions that people have posed about it.

"Is hypnosis used in this therapy?"

Definitely not, if by that term one indicates a trance state in which the subject is unaware of what is going on around him and can not return to normal functioning without the hypnotist's command. In our work the person is fully conscious, responding to questions in a very cognizant manner, but being aware of two "stratas" at once instead of only the usual beta-activity. (In a crude analogy it is like a person watching a movie while he is eating popcorn. He knows he is eating but he is vicariously living with the images on the screen.)

"How are the ideas taken from holography different from many popular techniques, some using muscle or nerve reactions to release subconscious blockages?"

Is there anything really "new"? There is one healing force and it takes place through many systems. Probably whatever a person selects, after investigation, is right for that person.

But he should be discriminating and make intelligent choices instead of submitting his mind to experimentation assuming that any method, especially if it is expensive, will be beneficial.

Holographic Therapy is in accordance with the most ancient, and most modern concepts of recognizing the *pattern* realm. How deeply imbedded it is in us is shown by the legends from Egypt where Poimandres tells Hermes (Toth), **"Before the visible universe was formed, its mold was cast.** This mold was called the archetype and was in the Supreme Mind long before the process of creation began."

The Hebrews taught that "God created man in His image—male and female created He them."[3]

Pythagoras taught that both man and the universe were made in the image of God; that everything observable in this world was a shadow or reflection, often distorted, of the universal pattern of perfection.

Even in India, thousands of years ago, the *Gita* informed people that "This body is called the Field and he who knows it is called the Knower of the Field. The Supreme (mind) which is without beginning—It shines through the functions of all senses and yet it is devoid of senses. It is unattached and yet It sustains all."[4]

Now, in the new physics, it is in agreement with Dr. David Bohm's Implicate Order, referring to the pattern world working itself out in the Explicate Order of the "thing" world. And, Prigogine's theory that there is a striving for a higher order of **complexity, counteracting the law of entropy, and** Sheldrake's "morphogenetic field" of formative causation. All of these concepts direct attention to the wholeness of all creation in the pattern realm.

For too long our methods of healing have dealt with band-aid types, treating the effect instead of the cause. An example that has been used is that of a radio which fails to perform. Work is done on the radio, taking parts out, replacing them and putting in new changes. The trouble may very well be that it is not tuned to a station. It may not be in the radio at all and no amount of tinkering with the electronic mechanism will produce the proper reception because the program is not produced in the set. It is created at the studio and transmitted to the set.

"Go to the source, the spring in the high mountain, and not the delta of the river if you would have pure water," the Sanskrit proverb reminds us. "Go to the Thinker and not the thought if you would have Truth."

EXAMPLES OF HOLOGRAPHIC THERAPY
Changing the Perspective or Attitude
A Canadian woman flew in for a Toning session, hoping to restore her singing voice. She had been unable to continue in her profession after a dreadful experience several years before. I felt that it was important to explore that before trying to work with her voice.

She had taken her little 6 year old son to the old village doctor for an immunization shot before school started. The child had a reaction to the drug, went into convulsions and died there in the office. She had taken in a healthy, bright little boy and carried out a corpse. The shock and grief had left a deep scar. And, she was unforgiving—the doctor should have tested for allergies before giving the shot—(how many thousands of children receive shots of all kinds without being tested?) She publicized it. The media took it up and it became a scandal across the country. The doctor lost his license and he died not long after. But her bitterness had not diminished. It was eroding her life as well as restraining her singing voice.

I helped her go into the alpha state and then asked her to visualize the old doctor sitting in the chair opposite her and tell him just how she felt. She began to denounce him for his carelessness. He was a murderer. She cried and yelled at him. Nothing bad enough could have happened to him for destroying her son's life, and her own. She raved on for perhaps 20 minutes. Then, tired out, she went into gentle sobbing.

The necessary emotion had been released. After a time I asked her to take the doctor's place and see the incident from his viewpoint. Still in alpha, she imagined herself to be the doctor. I reminded her of all the lives he had saved—babies delivered, the pain he had relieved, the blizzards he had gone through in the fierce winters to minister to the ill and dying. He had given his life to serving his patients and through no fault of his own, a boy had died. That was all people remembered. His whole life's efforts were erased by that one incident. He, too, had died because of that same accident—there was nothing more to live for.

She was quiet for a few minutes and then she blurted out, "Oh, my God! He suffered more than I."

For that moment she had changed places with the doctor. She saw the entire thing from another's viewpoint. Her facial expression changed and she looked 10 years younger. Bitterness and hatred were gone. We talked about it for a while, fastening the new viewpoint into her consciousness. Then she returned to her motel.

The next day she phoned. "Would you like to bring some friends and come to my room this evening? I'd like to give you a concert."

She had brought along a small auto-harp and that evening she sang for us—song after song in a lovely voice. I would guess it was more beautiful than it had ever been because now it had depths of compassion unknown before.

When she returned to her home she arranged for concert tours and also teaching in a college. That one session unlocked her imprisonment and she was free to live outside of a crippling illusion. Years later she is still touring, still singing and making her life a joy for others as well as herself.

That method of changing the perspective and seeing things from another's viewpoint has saved many marriages.

Changing the Feeling

I was giving some lectures in Philadelphia and had just an hour between presentations. A man, probably in his 40s, stopped me in the hall and implored me to see him. "I've got to have help. My wife has divorced me, my daughter hates me. I'm sure I'm going to lose my job and my health is failing. Please help me." After guiding him into alpha, I asked the key question; "Can you see the first time you felt you were not appreciated?"

"I was never appreciated. I tried so hard to please my father and he never knew I was around," he sobbed with a rush of tears.

He was the middle son of three. His father took the older and younger boys fishing, playing ball with them but ignored Martin. He continued, "I was always there when he was fixing things, handing him the pliers or rake or whatever and he just ignored me. It's been that way with my wife and the college where I teach—I just give and give and they just expect more and more."

I encouraged the shoulder-shaking sobs to continue for a time. Then I went behind his chair and drew his head back against me, stroking his hair from his forehead. "Listen to me," I said. "I am your father speaking to you. Listen. When your right hand does something for you, do you stop to thank it?"

"No, of course not." He answered slowly, a little puzzled at this strange questioning.

"That is why I never seemed to pay attention to you. You were so close to me, like my right hand. I never thought of thanking you. I felt you knew how much you meant to me because you were so close to me. The other boys were separate. You were a part of me."

Martin caught his breath and then sighed deeply. "Was that why?"

"Yes," I assured him. "Don't you see how it was?" I was talking to a little boy who wanted to believe. And he did!

I had no idea whether that was how his father felt or not. It didn't matter. That little boy was satisfied. The box had flipped! He was special. He was accepted. He was important.

"And," I put in another idea while he was in that receptive state. "Aren't you treating your body without appreciation?

Working it much too hard without appreciation for its needs?"

As we hurried back down the hall, he tried to thank me. "I feel so different—like tons of weight have fallen away. I can't believe it—"

Three weeks later he phoned to tell me that everything seemed to have changed. His attitude toward his work was very different and there was a possibility that he was up for promotion, and his health had improved since he was paying more attention to it. During the year I received brief notes but the best of all came at Christmas. A card, signed by him, his wife and daughter, (who had returned home) read, "That hour I spent with you in Philadelphia was the most profitable one in my life. Everything is so good now I can hardly believe it. I've just received a grant to do an important study that I wouldn't have thought of asking for a year ago. I can never thank you enough."

Replacing an Image

This case is one of the most dramatic we have encountered. Paul and I had been giving hologram therapy classes once a week for 5 weeks. The last night we gave techniques for dealing with problems, using visualization. After the class a beautiful, well-groomed woman came up to me and said, "You have no idea what an accomplishment it is for me to have walked up here alone to speak to you." She looked back, perhaps 20 feet, where her husband was standing, smiling happily.

Obviously, she was not crippled and my astonishment must have shown. She went on to explain, "I've had a phobia for 30 years. I can't go anywhere by myself—among other things."

Then she related an experience she had that night during one of our exercises.

"When you told us to visualize someone coming to help us, I saw Jesus—but suddenly my grandmother, who is dead, appeared and pushed Him aside and just stood there.

It frightened me. I'd like to talk with you about it."

We arranged an appointment and when her husband drove her up to see me she told me her unusual story. When she was 11 her grandmother had died, but she understood about death and it didn't seem to grieve her unduly. However, not long after that the fear of loose objects surfaced. A pin, a blade of grass on the floor, a cap left off a ball point pen, anything out of place kept her there until it was picked up or disposed of. At 16, while she was driving, a sports car whizzed around a corner and missed her car by inches. The terror was so real that she said she drove around the block several times, convinced that she would see her dead body there in the street. She could never drive again, nor go out alone.

The man who married her met her after these phobias had marred her life and he had taken care of her, driven her about, went with her wherever she needed to go and had become indispensable. He had done it most willingly for his love for her was evident.

She finished with, "You can't imagine what a hell you live in trying to appear normal when you think you're crazy."

She had tried many therapies, and done a great deal of study about her condition, without receiving help. I think she did not expect relief from her situation as much as she wanted to know why the visualization had been stopped by appearance of her grandmother.

She knew how to go into an alpha state easily and then I began questioning about her grandmother. There seemed to be no trauma there. That puzzled me. Then, an intuitive thought prompted me to ask, "Does this experience relate to something in this life or a previous one?"

Quickly, she responded, "Previous one."

(I do not wish to discuss the probability of reincarnation; prove or disprove it. I have seen, repeatedly, that if a person accepts it, it is a tool most effective. If it works, use it.)

I asked her to "Go back and see the incident that caused this fear—"

Before I could finish she began responding in a little girl's voice. Whimpering, she said, "But I'm little. I didn't know what to do. I'm little."

"What is happening?"

"My brother is crying and making funny noises."

She described him and the scene in detail. He was dressed in a little striped sailor suit with long black stockings. They were playing in a shed or shop-room apart from the main house.

"Why is he crying?" I asked.

"His toy broke."

"What kind of a toy broke?"

She explained that the wheel of his tiny toy wagon had come off and he was choking, apparently on the pin that had held the wheel in place.

"What is happening?" I persisted.

"My Papa is coming and he picks up Brother and scolds me, 'Why didn't you do something?" But I'm little—I didn't know what to do—" she sobbed.

"What does your Papa do?"

"He runs out with Brother—took him to the doctor—but I didn't know what to do. I'm just little—" she kept crying.

"What is happening now?"

She sighed. "Grandma comes in and she picks me up and holds me. She knows I'm little and I didn't know what to do. I couldn't help it."

Now I had a connection with the grandmother. When she had died, in this life time, this person had felt vulnerable. Her protection was gone and the guilt, that she associated with the brother's death in a past life, began to trouble her. Any small thing, a pin, a nail, a soft drink can tab—any small thing out of place was a threat to her. And, the near car accident when she was 16 related to wheels—out of control. The pieces of that illusion came together. Now we could replace that psychological hologram with another one.

I had her go back to the scene of the little brother choking, to feel the high emotion and fear again.

"Go over and hit him on his back—hard—and see what happens." (I was counting on her mature reasoning to reform this picture with good left-hemisphere logic.)

After a moment she said, "It flew out!"

"What did?"

"The thing from the wheel."

"Is your brother all right?"

"Yes, he's stopped coughing."

"What are you going to do now?"

"I'm going to pick up the piece and put it on the table and when Papa comes home he'll fix the wheel back on."

"See your Papa coming in and fixing it. Now, what happens?"

"Brother is playing with the wagon. He is happy, playing with it." She sighed deeply, indicating acceptance of that resolution.

"Everything is in its right place again," I urged her to repeat it with me. "Everything is in its right place and I am free. I am free—free—FREE." She had changed the past!

Then she began to tremble. She was back in beta consciousness and shivering, "I'm cold. I'm so very cold." It was almost as though she were going into shock. After all, she was turning around a conviction that had held her bound for 30 years and suddenly to have lost it would cause a radical adjustment to her entire being.

It was a warm spring day but she put her coat around her and huddled in it, shaking.

"You'll feel warm as soon as you go out in the sun," I assured her. "You've just had major surgery—but you're free. Keep feeling that."

"I know something amazing has happened. I feel—I'm light headed—and yet I feel so good—I don't know what happened. Could that be true—what I saw?"

"It provides some answers, doesn't it?"

"Oh, yes. It makes everything very clear. It must be true."

I walked with her to her car and asked her husband to take her to some restaurant that served hot Mexican food. (Such remedies are not to be found in psychological textbooks, believe me.)

It worked—it grounded her back into her body, I found, when I phoned her a few hours later. She was still wearing a fur coat but feeling strangely free.

The next day she got into their car, drove some 5 miles to her husband's shop where some equipment was being installed and there was metal strapping, nails, scraps of wood and trash all over the floor. She stepped over it with no concern and knew that she was indeed free. Her husband, realizing that she had driven there alone, almost went into shock. It was unbelievable to him.

I checked on her daily for a time—that is when I could find her at home. She was out driving much of the time. She was free and driving all over the city, doing things she had not done for so many years.

It was about 3 weeks later that she phoned. "We've got a problem," she announced, almost with humor in her voice. "It's my husband. He awakened me last night—very upset. He said, 'You don't need me anymore now, do you?' "

I was relieved. "That's your problem," I joked with her. "What are you going to do about it?"

"After all of these years of that dear man thinking of me and taking me everywhere, I've got to turn it around and remember to ask him to go with me!"

And, "they lived happily ever after."

While that healing was instantaneous, she did have to break the old habit pattern of those long years. When she became tired she noticed a tendency to slip back, but immediately she recognized it, she claimed her new hologram and chanted, "I'm free, I'm free. Everything is in its place and I am free." I had explained the shifting of the box to her and that she must hold her new memory of the occurrence until it was well established. To FEEL that whatever had happened belonged to another time. It was not *now*.

It's been nearly 4 years since that experience and she tells me it has been a steady growth of new awareness, a reshaping of her life, adjustments for her husband and children, (who had known her only as "different" from other mothers). But there has not been any relapse. She has remained free by accepting her replacement hologram as a valid memory from the past.

You Become Your Own Therapist

Holographic therapy is unique in that you become the healer. Whatever problem existed in your past can be treated because You-Now can deal with a happening in time, (other than "now.") You become the healer, the parent, the counselor for your previous selves. You would feel confident counseling a child or someone younger than yourself. In the same way you return in time to give comfort and reassurance to your little-self at earlier periods in life.

Dr. Irving Oyle has said that until we are about 5 we are largely dominated by the right hemisphere of the brain. At that age we are introduced to left hemisphere learning, and begin to develop reason, and linear thinking and seemingly cut off communication with the intuitive, creative right hemisphere functioning. It goes on trying to control the body but with little help from the person who grows up, and away, in his thinking world. The person may have a doctorate in science but over-eat, over-drink, over-work and wonder why he gets ulcers or heart attacks. It is that little 5 year old child-self in him that is trying to keep him from destroying the body. It can't get him to listen so it stops him in the only way it knows—illness or accidents.

When we use these holographic methods we are communicating with that little-self. Not all of the problems are created in childhood, or course. Some come in adult years but are accepted by that child-self and treated from that level. This often happens in marriage. The bride or groom do something that deeply disappoints the other because the person is not behaving as was expected. A hologram is created about it so the mate can see the other person only through that impression and never in any other light.

When you understand the techniques given here you can go back as the comforting, loving and understanding adult and change the condition that threatened the child-self locked in a time incident. (Remember the clock which was photographed on holographic film and past, present and future were all contained on the one plate?) By changing your perspective you realize that you are the Observer and you have control over those incidents in time through your choosing. You can be the parent to that child-self that it needs. Maybe that child felt unloved. Be the parent to it that you never had and feel the love you wished you had received.

Many people seem to feel that they were rejected or unloved by their parents. (No doubt most parents love their children but the little-child-self sees them from a naturally selfish perspective.) One young woman insisted that her mother had been so critical of her that she could never succeed in anything. She always "failed" just before accomplishing her goals. She felt that she could not graduate from college where she had been taking incompletes instead of finishing. We suggested that she replace her mother with another one—just the kind she wanted—who would support her, be proud of her, encourage her.

She was of Germanic ancestry and she envisioned a gentle Japanese mother who loved and encouraged her devotedly. Before every class and test, she imagined the new mother urging her on. She graduated, and felt confident of her future. About six months later she called, "That mother is so fine I'd like a new father too." We told her she knew how to create one if she needed one but suggested that it was time she grew up and became independent of a time frame of childhood.

As you change your perspective you realize that you have control over those increments of time. The pattern does not change but you are continually unfolding that which you are in reality; You-Now may also borrow from the perfection that you wish to be in your future. The more you hold attention on the ideal of yourself, the more you will hasten its manifestation. You can be now what you hoped to become. Just identify with that part of the time sequence, with that image. "Act as a saint and you become a saint."

This wisdom has run, as a silver thread, through all of the religions, though at times it seemed to have become sadly twisted and snarled or tied in hard knots.

In the *Gita*, Arjuna says finally, "My delusion is gone. I have regained my memory through Your Grace, O Lord. I am free from doubt. I will act according to Your word."[5]

Perhaps the "good news" the Christians based their religion on was a recognition of this pattern of perfection as holography reveals it to us now. It explains how that pattern could be in every person and no matter into how many fragments it may be separated, the perfect image, in which we were created, remains in each one. We need no longer take these ideas on faith. We can know them.

The "fall of man" could mean the fall of consciousness into the illusions of the senses and that was the "original sin" (separating our consciousness from Reality.)

No matter how many imprints, made with different colored lasers or positions, are on a film, if it is held up to pure white light all of the pictures disappear. If we hold our life-film up to the pure white light of "Love the Lord thy God with all of your heart and mind and soul," wouldn't all of our **hurts, traumas and mistakes (sins) be no longer visible**—and therefore "forgiven?"[6]

To put our attention on that original pattern and permit no more sense perception values to be stamped on our consciousness could mean to be "saved" from the suffering and guilts and problems that illusions lead us into. A scripture based on Truth has many levels of interpretation and perhaps these concepts would make those old, familiar stories more acceptable today.

Such ideas are in agreement with the natural laws of the universe as we comprehend it now. To have made them more useful to us, (through the ages and different stages of mind development in the past) names and personalities were given them—we made gods and devils of them but the majestic laws that rule the galaxies, and us, are from the One Great Pattern.

"Truth is one though men call it by various names."

THE UNFOLDING
HOLOGRAM OF LIFE

Just as each cell of your body contains a complete and detailed picture of you, so each of us is a cell in the body of the universe, with a complete and detailed picture of the Cosmos waiting to unfold.

6 What is an unfolding hologram?
It is a hologram in which a pattern is unfolding through time. The process of unfoldment implies motion. A movement not of the hologram but of the light shining on it. In a similar way we may have unfolded from embryos to adults. As we unfolded we experienced changes in our attitudes. As teenagers, we may have thought our parents were foolish and ignorant. As we became adults, we were astonished to see how much our parents had matured.

The illusion of time and space is perceived by looking through the hologram and seeing the image but the hologram itself is timeless. The observer has only to shift his attention to a different perspective in order to obtain the illusion of time (as seen in an earlier chapter, regarding the clock.) Left to its natural process, the single cell will unfold the original pattern to full maturity. However, this does not always happen now, because of radiation, poor nutrition and artificial environment.

Consider how nature intended it to be.

THE HOLOGRAPHIC SEED UNFOLDS

I remember as a child the first time I was introduced to the mystery of the seed. It was a warm spring day in May and my mother had worked all morning preparing the soil for our summer garden. To my surprise, she handed me a small package of corn seeds and told me to plant them so many inches apart and so deep. Carefully, I examined each kernel and looked up at my mother smiling at me. In a little boy's naivete I asked, "Will this little piece of corn make a tall stalk?"

"Yes," she replied.

"But how? I don't understand."

"When you plant the seed in the ground, the outer husk slowly rots away and the tiny pattern of a corn stalk and ears of corn inside it begin to unfold and reach for the light."

"You mean this tiny kernel has a stalk and lots of ears of corn in it, like we had last summer?" It seemed like magic to me.

"Yes, the pattern of the stalk and ears are in there and when we plant it and water and weed it, you'll see it will come up through the ground and grow tall."

"But what makes it big?"

"The same thing that makes you grow bigger. You have the pattern of a man in you, and the food you eat, and the things you learn and do all go to make you become what you ARE."

Little did I know that my mother was introducing me for the first time to the principle of the "Unfolding Hologram." What is the seed if not a fragment of the whole plant—in this case the corn stalk with its many flat leaves and ears of corn?

Each kernel has the pattern of the whole stalk of corn in it but we can't see it until it has unfolded.

Let's go over this seed idea again. The seed contains the pattern. Once that seed, in this case a kernel of corn, unfolds into a stalk, it creates more kernels and fastens them to the cob. It first *unfolded* the pattern of the kernel into a stalk, then *enfolded* the pattern back into each kernel, which in turn contains the pattern of all its corny ancestors.

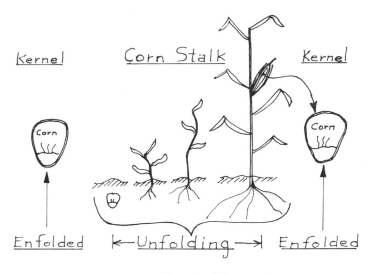

Figure 23

The cycle of corn is from kernel to stalk and back to kernel again; the process of all life.

I wish that I could claim credit for this astute observation but two very bright minds beat me to it. One was the late Itzhak Bentov, one of the really great thinkers of our time. He explains this concept in his book, *Stalking the Wild Pendulum*. In the book he uses the example of the tree and describes how the seed somehow codes the spatial and temporal form of the tree.[1] The spatial information pertains to its shape while the temporal pertains to the time sequence of unfolding the shape. I wonder if the tree had to take a graduate course in holography in order to know how to grow—under a government grant, of course.

The other exceptional mind at work on this idea of unfoldment is Dr. David Bohm, professor of Theoretical Psychics at Birbeck College, London University.

In his book, *Wholeness and the Implicate Order*, Dr. Bohm refers to this process of unfoldment-enfoldment as the "Holomovement."[2] He goes on to say that all entities are forms of the holomovement. Birth and death are merely transitions in the unfolding and enfolding universe. Nothing is ever really created or destroyed; merely unfolded and enfolded in the dance of the holomovement. It describes a holographic pattern in motion. Where else might we see this occuring in nature? In crystals. It is a very slow process and the crystal grows along a definite pattern structure. The pattern is found in the molecular form of the lattice and under a high powered microscope one can see the geometry of it.

Unless you still have a pet rock or two around the house this isn't a terribly exciting example but let us move on up the evolutionary scale to the animal kingdom.

THE HOLOGRAM AND DNA

Going back to our origin we find that we were originally a zygote in our mother's womb. The zygote is a fertilized egg that begins its life as a single cell. I know that is ego-deflating but we all began this lifetime as a single cell. Then how did we get where we are today?

We can blame it on mitosis. Somewhere between the moment of conception and birth that single cell divided and expanded so many times that it ended up as a human baby complete with arms, legs, head, eyelashes and fingernails. Look what nature did! In a single cell was the blueprint for a human body so incredibly detailed that even the color of the eyes and shade of hair was predetermined. The entire picture of a particular body was coded in that single cell. All that it had to do was unfold.

The pattern drew nourishment from a suitable environment and began to grow. After the physical body has matured, (unfolded) it enfolds its genetic pattern back into either sperm or egg. It is a very holographic process. These principles have penetrated the core of our being—our existence as a human depends on it.

If we put that single cell zygote under a powerful microscope, will we find the picture of the baby in it? (This was the concept of the sperm given by a 17th Century scientist.) *

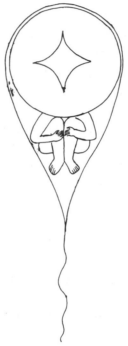

Figure 24

Under the microscope there is no such image. Not even genetic experts can see such a picture. But then neither can the expert holographer recognize the holographic image when analyzing a single fragment under the microscope with white light. The pattern still holds the picture in both cases.

* Reproduction of Hartseeker's drawing from *Essay de Dioptrique*, Paris 1694

Every cell contains the same genetic patterns. These patterns are grouped by the hundreds into single units called genes. Each gene has a specific trait, blue eyes or brown, color of hair, height and shape of the body, coded in the DNA molecules. The DNA is coded to manufacture the protein necessary to form blue eyes or brown, or whatever is required. String a few hundred genes together and you have a chromosome. The nucleus of each cell of the body contains forty-six identical chromosomes holding thousands of genes. (Each cell in my body has enough information to create an identical duplicate of me. The term used to describe such a process is called "cloning.")

Within the pattern of the zygote is the picture of a human body. As it unfolds, (mitosis) the picture takes on form. If we could tune in to the proper zygote frequency, perhaps we could see the form of a baby, as we can tune in to the proper frequency of a holographic fragment and see the whole picture.

Let us assume that we could tune in to the zygote and follow it through mitosis right up to birth. Would the pattern be changing? No. The pattern is fixed at conception. External influences can, however, inhibit or promote the unfoldment just as planting the corn kernel in a desert region would produce a scrawny plant, or in rich, fertile soil would produce an abundance of grain. In the desert it would struggle to grow but would not be fruitful. No matter where the corn was planted, it would never become a rose or a tomato, only a corn stalk.

Since we can describe the whole picture at any moment during its unfoldment, the pattern must exist outside the time domain. It works with time in unfolding, but as a pattern it is timeless.

Aha—now I see. The individual is complete in one domain (the pattern) even while a baby, but is not complete in the other domain (time) until he or she reaches adulthood. It takes time to unfold a pattern, but the pattern can be examined at any instant of its unfoldment, and it will still reveal the same basic figure.

While the original does not change, it does incorporate the experiences of its particular unfoldment. During the growth process, the pattern is revealing different aspects (perspectives) of its nature. Remember when we took a slice out of a hologram and the slice restricted our perspective of the overall picture? The larger the perspective the more comprehensive the picture became. Viewing the hologram slice from one angle revealed the pyramid and box, and from another angle we could see a ball as well. All three objects were there all of the time but the illusion of the unfolding picture (hologram) required that we shift our position in space to see other aspects of the whole. The original pattern did not change—only our perspective has changed. So the more perspectives of life we experience the quicker we mature. Experience doesn't have to be first-hand to be effective. I don't have to be a drug addict to realize the view of life that one gets from that lifestyle. The old adage, "What one observes and learns from observing, one does not have to experience," is still applicable.

The unfolding order of the seed is in reality an illusion. The PATTERN in the seed is the REALITY.

When we can read the whole pattern in the frequency domain, we do not need to wait for it to unfold in time. How does one read out the whole pattern in the frequency domain? The process involves "tuning in" and expanding, much like tuning the frequency or channel selector on a TV set.

Someone may object. "I'm confused. Isn't the real world that which is unfolding?"

Not according to the holographic concept. The unfolding images always fade away. Death, transformation through fire, destruction through disintegration—the unfolding form is always a victim of transitory conditions. The unfolded form has a limited life span; the pattern does not. If we are perfect to begin with what is the purpose of unfolding? In order to *see the larger picture*, the whole picture, and to provide an unlimited number of unique perspectives on the Holomovement we call Life.

HOLOGRAPHIC PATTERN IN EMOTIONAL NATURE

Does this process also apply to our emotional nature? Could it be that unfoldment takes place there as well? Let's explore this idea and and see if there is any evidence to support it.

As I look back on my own life, I realize that my emotional nature has gone through stages of growth or unfoldment. As a very young child, the basic emotions involved love of parents, fear of strangers, sometimes anger at my brother and others. As I grew older, feelings of companionship and love of the opposite sex began to awaken. In my early teens an appreciation for music began to unfold. That awareness had a powerful effect on my emotional maturity.

If we begin with the premise that there are certain basic emotions coded into our brains even before birth, then we become responsible for their unfoldment, or lack of it.

In Chapter Two we spoke of Manfred Clynes' work on "Sentic Forms", and how the human being tends to identify certain emotions with particular geometric patterns or forms. There seems to be a natural emotional response to these forms. Michelangelo's *Pieta* elicits the emotion of grief and compassion merely by its geometric lines and composition. In a similar way, his statue of *David* inspires strength, devotion and admiration.

Our emotional nature unfolds rapidly during certain critical stages of our life. Early in childhood, of course, and then at puberty. During those times, we should be especially alert to the emotional environment provided by music, literature, art and entertainment. Just as Thalidamide had a devastating impact on the developing fetus, so the emotional environment can play a major role in enhancing or damaging the process of emotional growth.

Most mothers, at this time, are aware of the importance of giving the youngsters good food, nurturing, and of letting them know that they are loved. But few parents provide guidance for their teenagers during that second critical emotional stage. Teenagers are left pretty much on their own, being allowed to make their own decisions when it comes to a musical diet. Without proper guidance, they feast on emotional junk food. Allan Bloom, University of Chicago, stated that the Rock beat appeals almost exclusively to the sexual longings of the young. "It caters to kiddy sexuality, at best to puppy love.—The motor of it all is eroticism."

Since music has a powerful formative influence on emotions, the quality of music becomes critical. From Beethoven to the Beetles and from Mozart to Punk Rock, the emotional impact is incredible.

Bach said of music, "It is the enlightened self-discipline of the various parts, each voluntarily imposing on itself the limits of its individual freedom for the well-being of the community. Not the autocracy of a single stubborn melody on the one hand nor the anarchy of unchecked noise on the other."

The prominant physicist, Dr. David Bohm, says "in listening to music, one is therefore directly perceiving an implicate order." If this is true, then the music can either reassure a person of the harmony and beauty of the ordered universe, or it can cause one to feel it is all a big sham.

This happens to be the way people relate when asked about their feelings toward the world while listening to various forms of music. Most classical and particularly Baroque music instills a feeling of well being, and that the world is a place of accord and order. Conversely, the attitude changes when listening to most contemporary music, especially rock and roll. The reaction is one of anger and resentment at the unfairness in the world. It appears that everyone is out to cheat and destroy the listener.

Over the past two decades I have observed an increasing insensitivity displayed by those in the rock music culture. The most noticeable characteristic of these people is their lack of emotional balance and control. They find it difficult to enjoy the subtle, refined ways of life. Their emotional natures appear to have been sadly crippled and malformed, and they can respond only to loud sounds and coarse feelings.

Music with a loud, pounding beat causes the body to respond as if it were in a constant state of "fight or flight." It has a weakening effect, generally, although people subjected to it regularly are unaware of its injurious nature, and as with any drug, seek more and more of it. Also, it is well known that among primitive people, the monotonous beating of drums puts them into trance states, where they can be manipulated easily.

Music was regarded in a very different light in other times. For instance, in India certain *ragas* were created to be used at certain times of the day, to be in harmony with natural forces. An evening *raga* was never played in the morning or a morning *raga* played at noon. That would have been out of rhythm with nature, (and God). In Plato's *Republic* Socrates made clear that he considered the control over music to be control over character. This was emphasized in the Pythagorean schools, music was divided into three parts; rhythm, melody and harmony. Rhythm was associated with the body, melody with the mental and emotional nature, and harmony represented the totality, or spiritual nature. Melodic, harmonious music is nourishment to the emotional nature in the same manner as certain good foods nourish the physical body.

HOLOGRAPHIC PATTERN IN THE MIND

In much the same way the mental pattern in each of us is undergoing a process of unfoldment. I recall my first years in grade school. The building was two stories tall and seemed enormous to me. I remember getting lost on the second floor, unable to find the room number. All in all, it was a terrifying experience. My mental nature was still in its infancy of unfolding. It grew, and as I moved on to second and third grades, the room numbers made sense. I could deal with new environments more easily. The thinking process was unfolding. The more I learned, the more the world was becoming organized. (The world wasn't changing, of course. I was.)

This mental unfoldment is nourished by school, teachers, books, associations and environment but there is a very important key which unlocks the natural process of mental growth. It is a combination of two essential qualities—CURIOSITY and the ability to OBSERVE.

Curiosity is the great developer of the mental nature. Without it unfoldment will be stifled, or at best forced and unnatural. It is the real motivation for all learning. Are you curious about life, its purpose and development for you? If you are not curious, but instead feel contented with your present answers, your mental nature is atrophying. It is not unfolding.

There is no age when we may stop asking, "Why?" It is one of the most magical words in our vocabulary. It makes life an exciting venture. There is so much we don't know, so much to be discovered, and these mysteries can be opened to us only if we insist on keeping our curiosity sharpened.

The second necessary aspect to mental unfoldment is the ability to observe. This may be an innate talent or it can be cultivated but without it we are seeing all of life in an opaque grey-zone. Observing is not analyzing. To analyze implies a series of comparisons, judgments based on rationalizing.

Observing means no pre-judging whatsoever; merely noticing, and seeing what is happening. To analyze is to project a theory or hypothesis upon the experience. To observe is to make a clear, definitive description of the event and its associated causes.

If one is curious and has the ability to truly observe, one can find the universe in a grain of sand or discover a myriad of products in the lowly peanut as Dr. George Washington Carver did. This brilliant black scientist displayed one of the finest examples of the curious mind with the ability to observe. While using these faculties he discovered a new world which other people had overlooked. In their narrow convictions they were so sure there was nothing that the peanut could be used for beyond the limits they had decided for it. Dr. Carver tuned into the pattern of the peanut and let it tell him of its potential for many uses.

Another example of this ability was Walter Russell, musician, artist, sculptor and scientist, who excelled in all avenues of expression he undertook. He received honorary degrees in those disciplines, although he never attended a college. Down through history we find records of a number of individuals who gained knowledge and wisdom through nonanalytical focusing techniques.

To tap into holographic patterns in the mind sounds incredulous, but it can be understood when we relate it to our TV sets. A set is designed to receive invisible low power electromagnetic waves. These waves are so weak that you have no idea they exist. However, just by turning the power on, and selecting a channel, you can pull pictures and sounds out of the air. The pictures were all around you but you couldn't see them until you tuned in. The process of tuning in to information anywhere in the world requires a carefully designed instrument such as a radio or TV. (It appears that our brain is equipped to do just that, when we direct it to do so.)

Dr. Carver, Walter Russell and others like them, apparently, have been able to do this because their minds could tune in to vast areas of knowledge of which the ordinary people were unaware—did not believe existed, and were not curious enough to try to explore beyond their accepted limitations. We have a marvelously constructed instrument in the brain and by directing the mind to choose, or tune in to a given object or area, that part of the universe will come to life for us. In a way, we are creating it by giving our attention to it.

Most of the world's greatest inventors and developers were inspired through their insatiable curiosity and exceptional ability to observe. Add these qualities to a broad spectrum of experience and you have all of the ingredients required for effectively unfolding your mental potentialities. All of the finest education in the world is useless if it doesn't stimulate curiosity and ability to observe.

It is my opinion that the greatest battles in the next few decades will be fought for the control of the mind. We hear of subliminal suggestions being given through sound and visual systems. We are vulnerable if we accept all that we see and hear in a passive, undiscerning manner, and if we have no value system by which to measure these inputs. Then the question arises, "How do I know what is true and not someone's opinion?"

A good standard of measurement is—when it is in harmony with the natural unfoldment we see in nature, and in agreement with the greatest minds down through thousands of years of history, it is most likely to be true.

There are numerous methods of mind control offered, and a simple question concerning them should determine their worth to us. "Does it enhance or *restrict* my mind?" Any structure, environment, teaching or doctrine that is based on restricting, or the limiting of one's natural tendency to question, is suspect. Such organizations and cults have one thing in common—they inhibit curiosity and freedom, and condition the person to see the world as they see it; "Our way is the only way. We are the only ones who have the truth." Holography proves that there are many perspectives and each is valid but some are more limited than others. The wise person tries to see the WHOLE PICTURE.

Each of us develops at his own rate and in his own time. One must follow one's own pattern. When we tune in to our natural pattern, everything seems to flow easily. When we are tuned out, everything seems to be an effort or go wrong.

PRUNING

In looking at this unfolding the natural pattern process, someone will want to use this idea to justify any behavior. "Sure, I stole the money. I was just unfolding my natural pattern," Or, "I ran him off the road. I had a right to express my anger. It's my emotional pattern unfolding."

Such attitudes are illusions. Take a wholistic view instead of a limited perspective.

Look at a fruit tree as it grows into a magnificent specimen, bearing abundant, luscious fruit. The trunk is sturdy and the branches strong enough to hold the weight of the fruit. It became that way by careful PRUNING.

That is the process of cutting back dead branches, snipping away the "suckers", (small shoots along the trunk that sap its energy and give no fruit) and shaping its early growth.

The question follows, "I can see cutting back dead branches but why shape the tree if it has the perfect pattern in the seed? Isn't it capable of unfolding without our help?"

In natural states they do grow according to their pattern as their environment allows. But, in our crowded societies where buildings, landscaping and orchards confine growth, pruning is necessary. Usually when a tree starts to grow it sends branches out in all directions. Left alone these early shoots can become so large and close to the ground that people or animals break them off as they move about them, leaving wounded areas open to insect infestation and perhaps death of the tree. Whether domesticated or in their wild state, when left untended, they are pruned by nature—storms, high winds and heavy snows. In the case of fruit trees, they produce much finer fruit when pruning is begun when they are young, and continued throughout their lifetime.

Human growth is very much like a tree. The process of pruning is essential in a child's development. It is called "discipline." (That does not imply punishment or repression. It comes from the same root as "disciple" which is to follow an example.) It helps shape the child's life for survival and self confidence, giving the fruit of happiness in return.

There are many people who have grown up without any pruning and the storms of life are twisting and breaking them. They are the ones who were told, that "if it feels good do it." The majority of those individuals are paying heavy prices to psychiatrists and counselors in attempts to remove dead timber or heal ugly, infected wounds in their bodies as well as minds and emotions. Those who can not afford professional help go on struggling to get through life one miserable day after another, feeling victimized. Some of them decide their only means of escape from their private hells is suicide.

Self discipline is the pruning shears we can use to shape our own genetic unfoldment. Without that the fruit we bear gets smaller and has less nourishment and flavor.

"But," someone will object, "isn't self discipline, by its very nature, restriction?"

Is the tree restricted by growing stronger and producing larger harvests of better fruit?

The choice each of us makes is—discipline or dissipation.

The human pattern can unfold in its inherent perfection when it is aided through proper guidance and loving assistance in the critical periods, setting a pattern for self-discipline as maturity progresses.

An inscription in the temple of Delphi in Greece so aptly puts it: "In all things, moderation." When we use self-discipline we find there is no need for the world "out there", or society or life itself, to prune us. That is freedom. That is unfolding in the true holographic pattern and enfolding the best back into our daily living.

UNFOLDING
THE PATTERN OF PERFECTION

"Throughout the universe there can be found a Natural Order which is forever unfolding. It unfolds to its perfection through the expression of love."

Count Nils Chrisander

7 If it is true that everything in the universe is in the process of unfolding it would be well to look at it in more depth. Just what are the stages of this process?

When we need an answer it can usually be found in nature. The design of the human body is a beautiful example. It has been unfolding its pattern for millions of years rather successfully. Observing the process we find there are four distinct stages.

> Intake
> Separation
> Assimilation and Regeneration
> Elimination

From the amoeba to the human being these four stages are inherent to unfoldment. Your own body follows this very sequence. You select food to ingest, your stomach breaks the food down through digestion, your intestines allow your blood to assimilate the nutrients and supply your body for regeneration, and finally your body eliminates the waste products. So long as each of these stages is allowed to function properly the original pattern will unfold in its perfection.

This process has its psychological counterparts as well.

Choice
Analysis
Integration & Transformation
Release

The entire process begins by making a choice and then the system automatically responds to it. Suppose you are wondering what to eat—you decide upon a carrot. (We will be health minded here.) You take the carrot into your system. You have made a choice. Next the stomach reacts to the carrot by breaking it down into amino acids, proteins and trace elements. Once this is done the digested food is passed on to the small intestine where these nutrients are slowly absorbed into the blood stream. Now the body can use the material to build, rebuild or repair its parts according to the pattern of health built into each cell.

Once the nourishment has been absorbed into the bloodstream, the remainder of that carrot is considered waste and is passed on to the larger intestine where it will be eliminated. This is the procedure that has allowed us to unfold as an "open dissipative structure," according to Dr. Prigogine.

Whatever substance, or pattern, is taken into the body must first be broken down, or separated, in order to be reorganized into the new pattern. This is how a carrot becomes muscle fiber or skin tissue. It is transformed in this growth process.

It is quite easy to interfere with this operation, however, beginning with the choice or intake.

CHOICE

Every experience we have had in this life is a direct result of our choices. This is a little scary to think about because it puts total responsibility on us for whatever comes into our life.

There is hardly a waking moment when you are not making a choice. You choose to read the next word or close the book, to remain sitting or get up, to make a phone call or eat, or drink something, for diversion. Even after making that choice, you choose HOW to react to it—with enthusiasm or reluctance, positively or negatively. Then you may spend time reflecting on the choices with satisfaction or regret.

Your physical condition, emotional state, environment, financial situation, relationships—all of these, and all that you have become, are simply the result of your choices. Your future is being made by the choices you make today. In this sense, you create your own life. Even if things beyond your control enter your life, still you create your *reaction* to them and in that you are in command.

There are people who would like to disclaim any responsibility for their parents or economic situation or physical condition. However, if we look more closely at the natural growth system, we may agree with Fred Wolf, who implies in his book *Taking the Quantum Leap* that there are no such things as victims in the world of quantum physics.[1] (Our bodies remain in a given form as a result of the laws of quantum physics so these laws apply to us.)

You may have encountered a situation which was very unpleasant but how you reacted was your decision. Any situation or circumstance that you might consider devastating, someone else would consider to be an opportunity. (Everything that you have and don't want, someone in the world would be delighted to have.)

This is not getting into "right" or "wrong" choices here—merely examining your power to choose an attitude toward a situation.

You have chosen your circle of friends over the years. Some have proved to be faithful, and a good influence, while others have been less than faithful and a detrimental factor in your life. In either case, you learned something from your choices.

As long as you see the connection between your choice and its effect on your life, the unfolding process will be enhanced.

Suppose you surrender your power of choice to another person or organization? You may sit back and relax while all of your decisions will be made for you. What will you learn from this? Very little, because you have taken no responsibility for the result of your decisions and your only response to a bad decision is to feel victimized. "They did it to me!" That is an illusion. You did it to yourself by surrendering your power of choice to some other authority.

"But, what about my parents?" you may ask. "Surely, I didn't choose them."

There are various perspectives from which to view that issue. Suppose that YOU, as a form of consciousness in some strata of existence, wish to unfold and realize that it can be done best through a certain environment. You may have chosen those very parents and circumstances because they provided the opportunity for growth that you needed. As we observe the many avenues that people take for their means of acquiring knowledge, it is like many schools with various curriculla. All of us have had to take a few undesirable courses from a few unlikable professors in an inadequate school facility in order to get the instruction we needed to graduate. It was not all perfect synchronisity but it was the best choice made available to us at that time.

Dr. Helen Wambach, in her book, *Life Before Life*, offers and interesting prospect in her study of over 700 case histories, using hypnosis and regression.[2] She took the subjects back through the womb to a period prior to conception. It appeared that many souls came into this world fully aware of the possible conditions and the choice was their's. In no case did she encounter a subject who, knowing what he or she was about to experience in this life, felt victimized by the situation. That attitude was fostered later by others who had accepted the "victim-illusion" and were intent on perpetuating the myth. An old saying is, "The only reason for making a wrong choice is to learn not to make it again."

To surrender your power of choice to anyone, or anything, is to stop the natural unfolding within you. Then, "How do we make wise choices?"

First, look at the result of other's choices. Ask yourself if you want the end result they have encountered. If not, don't make the associated choices.

Second, observe the effect of your choices on your well-being. Will they make you feel more secure, give you greater peace of mind and self-confidence, express your potentiality and give you the opportunity to "make the world a little better because you have lived in it."

When I say "observe", I mean see clearly. One cannot observe clearly if the brain is being affected by drugs of any kind. All drugs cause some form of distortion. And, we might place anything that does not nourish the body, but is taken in only for pleasure or stimulation, in the category of "drug."

Of course, some individuals may choose to put poisonous substances into their bodies. Even that choice is open to us. But, obviously, poison shuts down the unfolding process. Unfortunately, many people who are contaminating themselves, physically, mentally or emotionally, are not aware of it. Through ignorance, laziness and sometimes rebellion, they accept an illusion and it becomes an investment to them; they have put a part of themselves into it, and no one likes to admit having made a bad investment.

If one clearly observes how each choice has affected one's life, one can begin to correct future choices. Be discerning. Make intelligent judgments about the company you keep, whether it be people, music, art, literature or entertainment.

When one of our teachers was consulted by a person who was having all manner of problems, he asked simply, "Who have you been playing with?" It was a question that wise, old grandmothers used to ask a child when he came home with measles or head lice. It applies today in more abstract realms. If troubles, illness, misfortune and accidents seem to overwhelm a life, it is well to go back and view the associations that one has been keeping.

By these choices we create our own worlds. It is foolishness to let others create it for us. Take charge of your own life. It is your choice alone, to either unfold your plan of perfection, or someone else's plan based on *their illusions of who you are*. If your pattern is that of an orchid and someone decides that you belong in their cactus garden, your life-span will be cut short. And, to know what your real pattern is, it helps to understand the system of unfoldment that follows the choices that are made.

ANALYSIS

Once you have chosen to explore some experience in life, be sure to follow that experience with proper analysis. Another term that might be used here is "digestion." Both terms refer to separating or taking apart. (Remember, in the physical digestive procedure, nothing can become a part of bone and muscle until it is first broken down and separated.) Experiences should be analyzed to understand their content and value as nourishment. This is the digestive stage of taking nourishment from an experience. If you don't understand something that has happened to you and why it affects you the way it does, you can't begin to assimilate it into your pattern and benefit from it.

Some people seem to be starved for experiences. They will do almost anything just to feel a sensation. But, they never stop to digest what has happened so they keep repeating the same mistakes. At that stage of their unfoldment, they cannot distinguish between poison and nourishment. They just keep devouring exciting sensations. Because they are so mentally and emotionally famished, (although they would not admit it) they see no connection between their actions and the result of those actions.

This type of person desperately needs to analyze the cause and result of relationships manifesting in their lives, and for a while psychoanalysis appeared to fill that need. Where those techniques often failed, was in the next stage of unfoldment which involved transformation. People would get addicted to digesting experiences and forget to integrate the experience into their own pattern. They would analyze over and over, and make a game out of trying to uncover every cause behind every event in their lives. Instead of using what they found, being nourished by it, they left it there and found someone, or thing, to blame for their situation—keeping it outside of themselves. This prevented them from utilizing the nourishment contained in the experiences and so their unfoldment was interrupted. These are the people who are eager to tell you all of their ills and who or what caused them, but they feel helpless to do anything to correct them. Victims and martyrs. They seem to have forgotten, or were never aware, that they had a pattern to unfold.

INTEGRATION

The third stage of unfolding involves integrating or transforming into the pattern. Usually this occurs in the realm of feelings. We may have completely understood the cause and effect aspects of the situation but we cannot seem to integrate the outcome into our own pattern. We have to absorb the lesson learned by feeling "all right" or "complete"about it. One must learn to absorb the positive nutrients from any experience in order to unfold his or her true pattern. This involves letting the negative, or waste, portion pass away and be eliminated, from their consciousness.

Some people get this stage backwards; they try to absorb and live on the waste matter, (such as hatred, blame. fear, retaliation,) and eliminate the nourishment that was there for them. They poison themselves with these emotions refusing to let them go.

This is why hologram therapy emphasizes the importance of changing the feeling about a situation in order to get on with the growing process.

RELEASE

The fourth stage of unfoldment involves—letting go. It is that simple! Even nourishing food taken into the body has elements which are not needed. If these are retained in the intestinal tract, the body will begin to absorb them and become toxic.

Each experience in life, then, has aspects which must be released to promote the person's unfoldment. "That fellow did something unkind to me. I learned a lesson from it but some day I'll get even!" Such an attitude is an example of psychological constipation. Revenge keeps the person bound. The perfect purgative is forgiveness, mixed with a strong dose of gratitude for having an illusion exposed. A Hebrew professor explained that the word translated as "forgive" came from the Hebrew term, "to unshackle" and to be "freed, or unbound." That is a good point to consider—to forgive someone is to gain freedom from enslavement to him.

If you use these simple guidelines in your life, you will observe a natural unfolding of yourself into a healthy, happy and successful person.

CHOICE OF IDENTITY

Another way we have of fouling up the unfolding procedure is to forget, or never recognize, our true pattern. WHO/WHAT ARE WE? The capacity to forget seems to be uniquely human. The rose never forgets its pattern of "roseness." The dog never thinks it is an alligator. But humans often decide that they are weak, unworthy, victims, failures, and sometimes, animal-like. We tend to identify with patterns of imperfection more than with our true nature.

This came to me in a very graphic way when I was working with plants in my back yard. Each year I put fertilizer around the base of roses to produce more colorful and fragrant blossoms. The question came to me, "How could that odorous fertilizer make roses smell even more fragrant?"

I saw that example as the real miracle of unfoldment. No

matter what I put on it, the rose bush transformed it into its rose-pattern.

I imagined my rose bush talking back to me, as a human might, under similar circumstances.

"Don't put that stinking stuff around me! I want to be beautiful and give off a sweet fragrance. Please, don't do this to me."

The rose bush simply transforms the fertilizer and never for a moment identifies with the smell, or gives back a fertilizer odor.

Humans, however, have the ability to choose their identity. Pour some trouble or afflictions into their lives and they identify with it. They become the problem. "I guess I deserved to fail. I just wasn't meant to be a success." "No one in our family ever got the breaks. I didn't have a chance for a good education." Or, "It's God's will." (God gets blamed for all the wrong choices people make.) They separate their consciousness from their true pattern and become the fertilizer!

No doubt we do this because we aren't really sure who we are. We are told by some that we are sinners. They say we are evil by nature and only by the grace of God can we be changed into "good" people. This is in contradiction to a holographic universe. If we are born "bad" to start with, the entire design of the cosmos would have been erratic. No where else in nature do we see a seed start out being bad. Its pattern may be interfered with but its life impulse was for perfection. However, if it loses its identity with that pattern, it can develop malformations and even become destructive.

It seems to be more reasonable to accept the idea of being formed in a pattern of perfection but being born into ILLUSION (that is the original "sin", of missing the mark, or, as it is given in the Aramaic, "skidding off the true course.") Being "born again" is waking from the illusions and seeing REALITY.

YOUR UNIQUENESS

Every person on this planet creates a unique perspective of life. A doctor has educated himself to view the hologram of life from a perspective called "healing." An artist may view the hologram as a perspective of light and shadow, color and tone as a means of interpretation. A criminal may view his hologram through the perspective of "What is yours is mine. I got as much right to anything I want as you have."

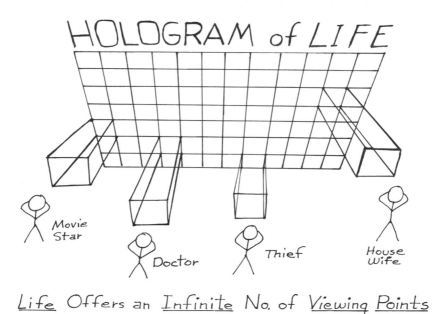

Life Offers an Infinite No. of Viewing Points

Figure 25

We come to see, through holography, that life is an unfolding process. There are an infinite number of perspectives available to view the process, just as there are an unlimited number of viewpoints for every hologram. That is what makes each of us so unique. The important thing to consider is not which is "right" or "wrong," but rather the degrees of limitation.

A limited point of view is just that—because of one's perspective, the view may be blocked and certain objects or conditions remain hidden until the person chooses to shift his viewpoint. (Again, the example of three objects stored on the hologram in figure 20). Some aspects of life are not visible when seen from a certain position. It does not mean that they do not exist. Simply, that they can not be seen from a particular fixed point of viewing.

We come to understand that in viewing life as a holographic image, we cannot say one point of view is true and another false. One can only observe the limitations of the perspective, or viewing point, that has been chosen.

This implies something very profound—*every experience in life is valid when seen from the context of the integrated whole.* By "integrated whole," I mean that each perspective, or fragment, has a unique place in the whole pattern. If one fragment becomes replaced, the whole pattern becomes disrupted like a jigsaw puzzle with the parts misplaced.

This is not unlike the process that occurs in brainwashing techniques, or mind manipulation. First the pattern of life is fragmented; the persons are subjected to psychological, and often, physical stress. Gradually their concepts and value systems begin to break apart. Then, the operator begins to rearrange these holographic fragments into a strange scramble of perspectives. The people are shown a hologram of life which is totally artificial and demands isolation to remain intact. This can result in such bizarre behavior as marching off with a group to drink poisoned kool-aid, at the command of an unbalanced instructor.

Be alert to anyone who is attempting to rearrange the integrated and natural order pattern of the whole, in order to confuse you and gain authority over your mental processes.

CHOOSING YOUR FREEDOM

We might compare the experience of life with the dream state. At night while we are dreaming we are lost in the illusion. The dream world is as real as the waking one. We are unconsciously creating the dream and then reacting to it, as though it were really happening.

Recently a new therapy technique has been developed involving lucid dreaming. The patients are trained to take control of their dreams and consciously change the outcome. This has a therapeutic effect because of the emotional release they experience in that dream state of having their life appear the way they wish it to be. Feeling fulfillment in that state carries over into their waking consciousness. This is an example of using the truth to deal with illusions. Using holographic principles we can achieve the same results in dealing with our every day illusions.

"Know the truth and the truth will set you free." Truth, then, becomes the instrument for attaining freedom. The whole concept of freedom and slavery could be related to what is called "good" and "evil." Traditionally that which we term "good" has given us freedom. That which we call "evil" has been a means to enslave us, so the garden of Eden story might have been written as "eating of the fruit of the tree of knowledge of freedom and slavery."

When people think of good and evil as being relative, they diminish the power of choice. Freedom and slavery are states of mind. They are not dependent on outward conditions. People in prisons may be "free," while others indulging their driving appetites for sensation are hopelessly enslaved, although being physically free. People living in confinement and regimentation in a government still have the freedom to choose to see a beautiful sunrise, to respond to a bird's song or hear water rushing over rocks, making its own music as it tumbles down a stream bed. Other people, living in a free country, may choose never to see a sunrise but only the ugly, and degraded.

THE POWER OF THE OBSERVER

In the holographic domain, we find three essential elements. The *Pattern*, the *Light* and the *Observer*. You and I, as the observers, find the pattern alone to be meaningless; the light alone invisible. The painting of the Mona Lisa in a completely dark closet could be considered worthless. It has no meaning until the light strikes it.

The light, too, has no meaning to us until it reflects off a pattern. If we look directly into the light we find the images disappear, as does the world of creativity. The creative process always has, and always will involve images.

That then leaves us with the necessity of combining light and pattern to produce images which can be observed, thus involving us in the creative process. Often, we forget our role as the observer and become attached to the images as did the slaves who were fascinated with the shadows dancing on the walls of Plato's cave. The result is suffering—deception, confusion and disappointment.

As we realize our error and attempt to escape suffering, we may renounce the images and become attached only to the pattern world. This leads to an intense investigation of the cause behind every event; the basic scientific approach. We believe that by understanding the pattern we shall know everything about it. But, as shown by recent discoveries in quantum physics, that is not the answer.

Still others may attempt to end their suffering and confusion by becoming attached to the light. This leads to a withdrawal from the material world. All material objects are diversions from God. One then renounces this world and withdraws to the cave or monastery. Complete devotion to the light and diety is all that is important. This may result in blind religious fervor where reason is forfeited to the belief that light alone is ruler. "God does this or that." "God punishes or rewards." Such believers feel that external powers control their lives. Some religions see all as *maya (illusion.)* Others personify their concept of the light as deity or devil. Each is true, in a limited way, but the truth lies in the *light of consciousness* which can illuminate all levels of patterns, bringing them to life.

The solution to this paradox seems to be with the OBSERVER. Only the observer has the magic key to this puzzle. He has the *power to be conscious.* Without this power being exercised, there may be no hologram, no image and no light.

Quantum physics is currently struggling with this problem. The observer has become the main ingredient in the equation defining reality. The observer may, in fact, be *creating the world merely by observing it.*

The key seems to be in that simple phrase: THE POWER TO BE CONSCIOUS, which is the greatest power in the universe. We think of the power of the sun, a bursting nova, even earthquakes and tidal waves, yet none of these have the power of choice. Humans do. We have the power to stop the sun in our sky and cause our earth to turn—all without moving a finger!

By developing this power to its ultimate potential we can illuminate and observe the infinite levels of patterns in our worlds, allowing us to see through the illusions of separateness and suffering, and become masters of our lives.

Whenever this Power To Be Conscious finally breaks through the illusions and glimpses the pattern of perfection in its totality, a strange thing happens. The individual begins to talk about "everything being in its right place", about being "born again" into a new understanding, about seeing the "unity and oneness of all life", and about an overpowering feeling of "love for all living things".

Some call this experience God Realization. By whatever name you choose to call it, the experience remains a deep and integral part of one's being. If it hasn't happened to you yet, don't worry, it will. It must, because this is the goal of all consciousness and it is inevitable. This then is the purpose of life - - - to allow the unfolding of consciousness to its ultimate potential and in the process cause the universe to unfold.

To be continued, because there are other perspectives yet to be explored—

NOTES

Chapter 2

1. Karl Pibram, *Languages of the Brain* (Monterey, Calif.: Brooks/Cole Publishing Co. 1977), page 169.

2. Peter Tompkins, *Secrets of the Great Pyramid* (New York: Harper & Row, Publishers 1971), page 192.

3. Manly Hall, *The Secret Teachings of All Ages* (San Francisco: H. S. Crocker Company Inc. 1928), page 82.

4. Lowell Hart, *Satan's Music Exposed* (Huntingdon Valley, Penn.: Salem Kirban Publishers 1981), page 61.

5. John Diamond, *Behavioral Kinesiology* (New York: Harper & Row Publishers 1979), pages 100—105.

6. S. Ostrander and L. Schroeder, *Super Learning* (New York: Dell Publishing 1979), pages 112—114.

7. Gabrielle Brown, *The New Celibacy* (New York: McGraw-Hill 1980), pages 33, 34.

Chapter 3

1. Arthur Klein, *Holography* (New York: Lippincott Company 1972), page 156.

2. Fred Wolf, *Taking the Quantum Leap* (New York: Harper & Row Publishers 1981) page 105.

3. M. Tekulsky and L. Asinof, "Holography—Laser Pictures That Live," Science Digest (July, 1981): 49.

4. Michael Wenyon, *Understanding Holography* (New York: Arco Publishing 1978), page 119.

5. *"3-D whole-body holographic scanner,"* RNM Images, April 1984, page 32.

6. Kenneth Ring, *Life at Death* (New York: Coward Mc-Cann & Geoghegan 1980) Chapter 12.

Chapter 4

1. Karl Pribram, "The Neurophysiology of Remembering," Scientific American (January, 1969).

126

2. Karl Pribram, *Language of the Brain* (Monterey, Calif: Brooks/Cole Publishing Company, 1977), chapter 8.
3. Marilyn Ferguson, "Karl Pribram's Changing Reality," Human Behavior (May 1978).
4. Daniel Goleman, "Holographic Memory," Psychology Today (February, 1979).
5. Judith Hopper, "Interview—Karl Pribram" Omni (October, 1982), page 129.

Chapter 5
1. Arthur Klein, *Holography* (New York: Lippincott Company 1972), page 156.
2. Marilyn Ferguson, *The Aquarian Conspiracy* (Los Angeles: J.P. Tarcher Inc., 1980), page 169.
3. Bible quote — Genesis 1:27
4. Bhagavad Gita — Chapter 13: 1 through 34
5. Ibid., Chapter 18:73.
6. Bible quote — Mathew 22:37.

Chapter 6
1. Itzhak Bentov, *Stalking The Wild Pendulum* (New York: E.P. Dutton 1977), page 115.
2. David Bohm, *Wholeness And The Implicate Order* (Boston: Routledge & Kegan Paul), page 150—7.

Chapter 7
1. Fred Wolf, *Taking The Quantum Leap* (New York: Harper & Row Publishers), pages 141—6.
2. Helen Wamback, *Life Before Life* (New York: Bantam Books Inc. 1979), page 62.

BIBLIOGRAPHY

Augros & Stanciv. *The New Story of Science*. Illinois: Gateway Editions, 1983.

Bach, Richard. *Illusions*. New York: Dell Publishing, 1977.

Bentov, Itzhak. *Stalking The Wild Pendulum*. New York: E. P. Dutton, 1977.

Bohm, David. *Wholeness And The Implicate Order*. Boston: Routledge & Kegan Paul, 1980.

Briggs & Peat. *Looking Glass Universe*. New York: Cornerstone Library, 1984.

Cade, Maxwell and Nona Coxhead. *The Awakened Mind*. New York: Dell Publishing, 1979.

Capra, Fritjof. *The Tao of Physics*. Berkeley, Calif.: Shambhala, 1975.

Clark, Glenn. *The Man Who Tapped The Secrets of The Universe*. Waynesboro, Virginia: The University of Science and Philosophy, 1946.

Clynes, Manfred. *Sentics — The Touch of Emotions*. Garden City, New York, 1977.

Clynes, Manfred. *Music, Mind and Brain: The Neuropsychology of Music*. New York: Plenum Press, 1982.

Conway, Flo and Jim Siegelman. *Snapping*. New York: J.B. Lippincott Co., 1978.

Deikman, Arthur. *The Observing Self*. Boston: Beacon Press, 1982.

Diamond, John. *Behavioral Kinesiology*. New York: Harper & Row, 1979.

Dossey, Larry. *Space, Time & Medicine*. Boulder, Colorado: Shambhala, 1982.

Drake, Henry. *The People's Plato*. New York: Philisophical Library Inc., 1958.

Ferguson, Marilyn. *The Aquarian Conspiracy*. Los Angeles: J.P. Tarcher Inc., 1980.

Gendlin, Eugene. *Focusing*. New York: Everest House, 1978.

Greguss, Pal. *Holography In Medicine*. Gildford, Surrey, England: Science and Technology Press Ltd., 1973.

Halpern, Steve. *Tuning The Human Instrument*. Palo Alto, Calif.: Spectrum Research Institute, 1978.

Kock, Winston. *Lasers And Holography*. New York: Dover Publications Inc., 1981.

Keyes, Laurel and Paul Chivington. *What's Eating You?* Marina del Rey, Calif.: DeVorss & Co., 1978.

Keyes, Laurel Elizabeth. *Toning—the Creative Power of the Voice*, Marina del Rey, Calif.: DeVorss & Co., 1973.

Moody, Raymond. *Life After Life*. New York: Bantam Books Inc., 1975.

Pierce, Joseph Chilton. *Bonds of Power*. New York: Bantam Books, 1982.

Pierce, Joseph Chilton. *Magical Child*. New York: Bantam Books, 1977.

Pietsch, Paul. *Shufflebrain*. Boston: Houghton Mifflin Co., 1981.

Pribram, Karl. *Languages Of The Brain*. Monterey, Calif.; Brooks/Cole Pub., 1977.

Prigogine, Ilya. *From Being To Becoming*. San Francisco: W.H. Freeman and Co., 1980

Restak, Richard. *The Brain The Last Frontier*. New York: Warner Books, 1979.

Retallack, Dorothy. *The Sound Of Music And Plants*. Marina del Rey, Calif., DeVorss Press, 1973.

Ring, Kenneth. *Life At Death*. New York: Coward, McCann & Geoghegan, 1980.

Schul, Bill. *The Psychic Frontiers Of Medicine*. Greenwich, Connecticut: Fawcett Publications Inc., 1977.

Schul, Bill and Ed Pettit. *The Secret Power Of Pyramids*. Greenwich, Connecticut: Fawcett Publications Inc., 1975.

Sheldrake, Rupert. *A New Science Of Life*. Los Angeles: J.P. Tarcher, 1981.

Talbot, Michael. *Mysticism and New Physics*. New York: Bantam Books, Inc., 1981.

Targ, Russell and Harold Puthoff. *Mind-Reach*. Delacorte Press/Eleanor Friede, 1977.

Tompkins, Peter. *Secrets of the Great Pyramid*. New York: Harper & Row, 1971.

Vitvan. *The Problem of Good and Evil*. Santa Barbara, Calif.: Rowney Press, 1952.

Wambach, Helen. *Life Before Life*. New York: Bantam Books Inc., 1979.

Wenyon, Michael. *Understanding Holography*. New York: Arco Publishing Co. In., 1978.

Wilber, Ken. *The Holographic Paradigm*. Boulder, Colorado: Shambhala, 1982.

Wolf, Fred. *Taking The Quantum Leap*. New York: Harper & Row, 1981.

Zukav, Gary. *The Dancing Wu Li Masters*. New York: William Morrow And Co. Inc., 1979.